MYTHOLOGY AND CULTURE WORLDWIDE

Aztec Mythology

DON NARDO

LUCENT BOOKS

A part of Gale, Cengage Learning

GALE
CENGAGE Learning

Farmington Hills, Mich • San Francisco • New York • Waterville, Maine
Meriden, Conn • Mason, Ohio • Chicago

© 2015 Gale, Cengage Learning

WCN:01-100-101

LIBRARY OF CONGRESS CATALOGING-IN-PUBLICATION DATA

Nardo, Don, 1947-
 Aztec mythology / by Don Nardo.
   pages cm -- (Mythology and culture worldwide)
 Includes bibliographical references and index.
 ISBN 978-1-4205-0922-9 (hardback)
 1. Aztecs--Folklore. 2. Aztec mythology--Juvenile literature. I. Title.
 F1219.76.F65N37 2014
 398.208997'452--dc23

                                                                    2014021883

Lucent Books
27500 Drake Rd.
Farmington Hills, MI 48331

ISBN-13: 978-1-4205-0922-9
ISBN-10: 1-4205-0922-5

Printed in the United States of America
1 2 3 4 5 6 7 19 18 17 16 15

TABLE OF CONTENTS

Map of the Aztec Civilization

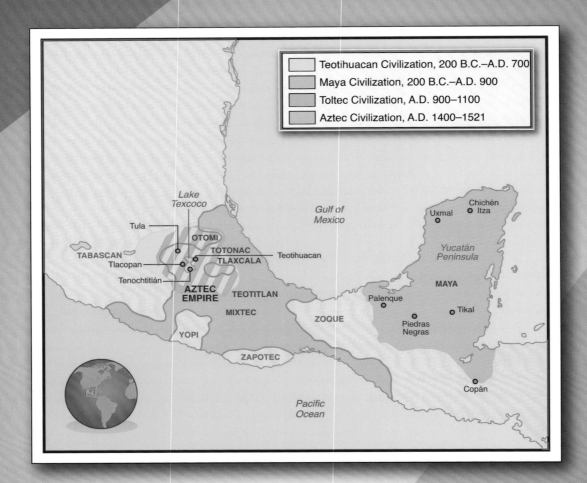

Major Entities in Aztec Mythology

Character Name	Pronunciation	Description
Chalchiuhtlicue	Chal-chyoot-LEE-kweh	The goddess who oversaw lakes, seas, and rivers.
Cihuaoatl	see-wah-OH-uh-tl	The goddess of midwives and protector of women who died in childbirth. She helped Quetzalcoatl create a new human race.
Coatlicue	koh-aht-LEE-kweh	A mother goddess said to have made the moon and stars.
Huitzilopochtli	weet-zil-oh-POCH-tlee	A war god and the Aztecs' patron deity, who helped them migrate to the Valley of Mexico.
Mictlantecuhtli	mikt-lan-teh-KOOT-lee	The lord of Mictlan, the underworld, where many of the souls of dead people ended up.
Nanahuatzin	nah-nah-WAT-sin	Originally the deity who oversaw skin diseases, like leprosy, he sacrificed himself to ensure that humanity would survive and then became the sun god.
Olmecs	OHL-meks	The first Mesoamerican people to build an advanced civilization, they set many of the cultural standards followed later by others, including the Aztecs.
Ometeotl	oh-meh-tee-OH-tl	A deity of fire and light, he was also the original and most powerful creator god.
Quetzalcoatl	keht-sul-koh-AH-tl	One of the principal Aztec creator gods, as well as the god of the winds.
Tecuciztecatl	teh-kuh-sis-TAYK-uh-tl	Originally the god of seashells, he was one of the first two gods to sacrifice his life for humanity.
Teotihuacanos	teh-oh-tee-wuh-CAHN-ohz	A mysterious Mesoamerican people who built the vast city of Teotihuacán in central Mexico centuries before the Aztecs appeared.
Tezcatlipoca	tes-caht-lee-POH-kah	An important creator deity and a war god with a dark, unpredictable personality.
Tlaloc	t'LAH-lok	The god of rain.
Toltecs	TOHL-teks	An important Mesoamerican people who preceded the Aztecs in central Mexico.
Xipe Totec	shee-peh-TOH-tek	One of the early creator gods and the bringer of spring rains.
Xochiquetzal	shoh-chee-KAY-tsal	The goddess of flowers, corn, and sexual desire.
Xolotl	SHOH-luh-tl	Quetzalcoatl's faithful dog, who accompanied him on his perilous journey to retrieve the bones of humans.

Altering the Past to Explain the Present

The Aztecs were the last major native people of Meso-america (ancient Central America) to thrive before the European conquest of that region in the 1500s. Like most other premodern peoples around the globe, they had a collection of rich and colorful myths about the creation of the world and humanity and the early deeds of gods they worshipped. It has recently become clear to modern scholars that the Aztecs did something somewhat unusual with one of their most important myths. Namely, they changed its story in the years following the conquest, after it had been well established and largely unchanged for centuries.

When the World Was Young

Before examining that myth and the reasons the Aztecs changed it, it is first essential to understand the more customary manner in which the world's cultures have viewed and treated their myths. The stories told in those myths are almost always set far in the past. Usually that past exists hundreds or thousands of years before "the present day" of the people or nation recalling or celebrating those legends.

The famous myths of the ancient Greeks are a good example. For the Greeks who defeated the Persians at Marathon and erected the magnificent Parthenon temple, "the present" was the fifth century B.C., during Greece's so-called Classical Age. They had a veritable treasure trove of myths that are still retold and enjoyed today. Among them are the timeless tales about Achilles, Odysseus, and the other heroes of the Trojan War, and the adventures of Zeus, Athena, and their fellow gods who dwelled atop towering Mount Olympus.

The Classical Greeks were unanimous in their belief that the events of those widely cherished stories happened in the remote past. The same was true of the Babylonians, who fondly remembered their ancient hero, the wrestler-king Gilgamesh; centuries later the Romans, who looked back with pride at the foundation of their race by the warrior and wanderer Aeneas; and later still the British, who recalled the gallant knights of Camelot, led by the legendary King Arthur. All of these characters and their deeds inhabited a dimly remembered world. As the renowned early modern mythologist (myth collector and teller) Edith Hamilton put it, the "real interest" in myths "is that they lead us back to a time when the world was young and people had a connection with the earth, with trees and seas and flowers and hills unlike anything we ourselves can feel. When the stories were being shaped, we are given to understand, little distinction had as yet been made between the real and the unreal."[1]

Hamilton's point that the unreal blended with the real in ancient myths is crucial. Indeed, what today are seen as fanciful interactions between humans, gods, giants, and monsters were, in the worldview of the peoples who regularly recalled those tales, often considered memories of very real past events. Thus, many Classical Greeks firmly believed that the Trojan War had been an actual event and that the goddess Athena had really emerged, wearing full armor, from the head of her father, the divine Zeus.

Ethical Opposites

Many ancient, medieval, and even some early modern peoples believed not only that the events of their myths were real, but also that some of those tales could explain or even predict future events. A well-known Norse (Viking) myth, for example, foretells that in the far future the gods will do

The Aztec god Quetzalcoatl, shown at right as a serpent, represented light and goodness, while Tezcatlipoca, left, stood for darkness and evil, and each exerted an equally powerful hold on the Aztec mind, imagination, and religion.

battle with evil creatures; and despite their great courage and strength, the gods will lose, thereby bringing about the end of the world as people have long known it. Similarly, Hindu mythology mentions long ages called Yugas. According to various Hindu accounts, the presently ongoing Yuga will end several thousand years hence, although exactly what will happen when it ends is open to wide interpretation.

Similarly, the Aztecs had a myth that seemed to foretell future events. It involved two major gods from their extremely large pantheon (group of gods)—Quetzalcoatl and Tezcatlipoca. These deities were thought to despise each other, in large part because they stood for ethical opposites. Quetzalcoatl represented light and goodness, whereas Tezcatlipoca stood for darkness and evil, and each exerted an equally powerful hold on the Aztec mind, imagination, and religion.

Quetzalcoatl, often called the Feathered Serpent, was god of the winds and a potent deity of healing. He was also the patron god of priests and artists and a mighty storehouse of wisdom, love, and truth, as well as the founder of the office of kingship on earth. Regarding that last attribute—creator of kingship—the Aztecs recognized a human manifestation of Quetzalcoatl, called Topiltzin Quetzalcoatl. The belief was that he had been the first great ruler of the Toltecs. (A people who existed several centuries earlier, they were seen then, and are still viewed today, as key predecessors of the Aztecs and other Mesoamerican peoples encountered by Spaniards in the 1500s.)

In a way, the heroic Topiltzin Quetzalcoatl was to the Aztecs as King Arthur was to the early modern British—the leader of a once great ancient realm. Just as Arthur eventually departed for a legendary land (Avalon), Topiltzin Quetzalcoatl left Mexico and sailed away toward the east. There, according to some accounts, he became one with his divine counterpart, the god Quetzalcoatl.

Meanwhile, that deity's heavenly opponent, Tezcatlipoca, whom the Aztecs called Smoking Mirror, was a sinister and mean-spirited creator deity. A dark, shadowy character, he was given to violent outbursts, and that tendency toward aggression showed itself in his role as the Aztecs' chief war god. Inspired by him, they came to believe that their destiny was to use warfare as a way of asserting themselves and achieving success. Mythologists Werner Forman and C.A. Burland explain, "To the people of ancient Mexico, there was no question that war was a duty, and that [neighboring peoples] must strive to control one another. It was fully accepted that the patron gods of the [various peoples] were the victors in the struggle, and those that died, died for the honor of their gods."[2]

An Error in the Natural Order?

An important aspect of the myth was that Tezcatlipoca, in his hatred for Quetzalcoatl, tricked Topiltzin Quetzalcoatl into getting drunk and disgracing himself in front of his subjects. This was the reason that the Toltec king left Mexico for the east. In a very real sense, he banished himself out of shame.

Even more critical to the story was a prediction that Quetzalcoatl would return to Mexico someday to reclaim his power as a monarch of that region. So when the Spaniards appeared in 1519, the Aztec ruler, Motecuhzoma, thought that their intrepid general, Hernán Cortés, was the god returning at last. As a result, the Aztec king was too trusting of the newcomers, who thereby steadily gained the upper hand and utterly defeated the locals.

That version of the Aztecs' fall, in which their myth about two opposing gods played a major role, was accepted by the vast majority of scholars up to the last couple of decades of the twentieth century. As late as 1975, one expert stated that "the strange story of the conflict between the gods Feathered Serpent and Smoking Mirror largely determined the actions of the Aztec people when, in the early sixteenth century, the Spanish invaders brought the era of native rule to an end. At this point, history and mythology united for a moment to produce a great tragedy."[3]

As it turned out, however, a more careful study of the Aztec myths and writings in the 1980s and 1990s revealed an important inconsistency. No preconquest native sources mentioned anything about Quetzalcoatl promising to return to Mexico in the future. That and some other related details of the myth appeared only in writings penned in the decades immediately *after* the Spanish invasion. These aspects of the story seem to have been added with the intent of changing the basic meaning of the myth so that it better explained why Motecuhzoma made the glaring mistakes that led to the Aztecs' fall. That ruler's actions "so puzzled and troubled" a group of his nobles, says Michael E. Smith, a leading expert on the Aztecs,

> that after the conquest they contrived a story to account for them. First, they created an "ancient" prophecy which stated that the god-king Quetzalcoatl would return from across the eastern sea to rule Mexico in the year 1 acatl, or 1519. Next, they invented a series of omens and signs that pointed to the coming of Quetzalcoatl. Finally, they claimed that Motecuhzoma truly believed Cortés to have been the deity himself. In the context of this story, Motecuhzoma's hesitation made sense. He thought that the arrival of the Spaniards was the second coming of Quetzalcoatl, not an invasion of strange foreigners.[4]

The problem was that the Spanish priests who wrote down the surviving Aztec myths in the generation following the conquest did not know that the myth in question had been revised after Motecuhzoma's death. So for more than four centuries historians assumed that that ruler's actions were in large degree the result of his interpretation of an ancient myth. According to noted scholar Susan D. Gillespie, who has closely studied this case of manipulating an existing myth, the past was "altered to conform to and to be continuous with the present." Indeed, she states, real Aztec history "was transformed so that it could accommodate the events of the conquest."[5]

It should be pointed out that the Aztecs who "transformed" the myth probably did not see it as a sneaky or fraudulent act. In all likelihood, they were deeply disturbed by their ruler's failure to stop the conquest, as well as by the fact that their existing myths had not foretold the Aztec

Hernán Cortés meets Motecuhzoma. After the conquest, the Spanish priests wrote that Motecuhzoma believed Cortés to be the second coming of the god Quetzalcoatl.

Empire's fall. They may well have concluded that altering the Quetzalcoatl myth was a logical and necessary way to correct what they saw as an unexplainable error in the natural cosmic order. If Motecuhzoma believed that Cortés was the returning god, the king's trust of Cortés and the subsequent Spanish victory made sense. By altering the past to explain the present, a small group of Aztecs demonstrated how seriously they viewed their myths and the potent power these tales held over their minds.

CHAPTER 1

Enchanted Vision: The Aztecs and Their Gods

When the Spaniards under Hernán Cortés arrived in Mexico in 1519, they were surprised, even startled, at what they found. Instead of groups of simple, loosely organized hunter-gatherers and farmers, as they had recently encountered in Cuba and other nearby islands, they discovered a large-scale, well-organized empire. It stretched from Mexico's Atlantic coast westward to the Pacific Ocean and contained about 5 million people.

That realm, which in size and complexity rivaled several that had developed in Europe, was controlled by a people who called themselves the Mexica (from which the term *Mexico* derives). This was the term that Cortés and other Europeans used for them for almost three centuries. Only in 1810 did this change, when German naturalist Alexander von Humboldt coined the name *Aztecs* to describe them and other natives of central Mexico. That new name stuck, and thereafter most people called the Mexica the Aztecs. The Spaniards found that the Mexica were not only organized and militarily strong enough to create and maintain a far-flung empire but that the natives also had a central capital, Tenochtitlan (teh-noch-teet-LAHN), that covered 5 square miles (13 sq. km) and had at least two hundred thousand inhabitants. Some quick calculations showed that these attributes made it the fourth-largest city in the world, after Paris, Venice, and Constantinople. This fact alone stunned many of Cortés's soldiers. The Spaniards were also mightily impressed by the huge size of some of the city's buildings and the overall high level of planning and engineering involved. Tenochtitlan stood on an island in a huge lake, called Texcoco, and was connected to the mainland by three stone causeways, or elevated roads, one of them 5 miles (8 km) long. According to one Spanish soldier, Bernal Diaz del Castillo, when he and his countrymen saw the city "and level causeways leading to [Tenochtitlan], we were astounded. These great towns and [temples] and buildings rising from the water, all made of stone, seemed like an enchanted vision from the tale of Amadis [a romantic adventure story then popular in Europe]. Indeed, some of our soldiers asked whether it was not all a dream."[6]

The Spaniards soon found that the Mexica possessed another important example of high culture—writing, which had allowed them to amass large numbers of books. One of the highlights of that Aztec literature was a collection of myths that explained how the world, human society, and the Aztecs themselves had come to be. There were also myths that explained the origins of practically every aspect of everyday life. For instance, some stories told how gods or goddesses had long ago introduced humans to concepts like love and beauty, and other myths showed people how they had learned to grow corn and other foods, make clothes, and so forth.

Myths About Past Peoples

For the Aztecs, therefore, myths were not fanciful stories, but rather pieces of history that gave their civilization a supporting foundation and connected them to both nature and the gods. Regarding that historical foundation in particular, certain myths described the Aztecs' predecessors in the region and explained why and how they had disappeared, opening the way for the rise of the Aztecs themselves. The creation of such legends was both natural and necessary because the huge region of central Mexico in which the Aztecs and their neighbors lived was littered with the ruins of cities erected by past peoples. In fact, modern archaeologists have verified that several other culturally advanced

Mesoamerican peoples had occupied the region before the Aztecs.

The first major example was the emergence of urban centers (cities) under the Olmecs, a people who thrived between 1800 and 300 B.C. Evidence shows they created the cultural model—including architecture, arts, clothing styles, military customs, and so forth—for most later Mesoamerican peoples. Among those other pre-Aztec groups were the Zapotecs, Maya, and Teotihuacanos.

The Teotihuacanos were named for their vast city of Teotihuacan, situated northeast of Lake Texcoco. Covering an incredible 12 square miles (20 sq. km), it featured a central ceremonial area with more than one hundred temples, shrines, and altars. The Aztecs called the largest temple-pyramid, towering to an amazing 246 feet (75m), the Pyramid of Sun. At the time, they had no way of knowing it was the third-most massive pyramid in the world, after Egypt's two largest.

In fact, the Aztecs and other later Mesoamerican peoples knew precious little about the Teotihuacanos, who had mysteriously disappeared in the eighth century A.D., abandoning their immense city. Yet their influence remained strong, as the Aztecs saw Teotihuacan as sacred and special. To them, it was the birthplace of the gods, as described in one of their most important myths. To commemorate that ancient, divine event, groups of Aztecs made periodic journeys to the gigantic ghost town. Standing in the enormous, once crowded but now deserted plazas, they likely saw the events of that myth play out in their mind's eye.

Another important pre-Aztec people in the region, the Toltecs, were also leading subjects of Aztec myths. Indeed, the Aztecs viewed the abandoned Toltec capital of Tollan (their name for the site now called Tula, lying 50 miles [80 km] north of Tenochtitlan) as "a fantastic city of mythical proportions and qualities," in Michael E. Smith's words. Groups of Aztecs made pilgrimages to Tollan, as they did to Teotihuacan, to witness

Gods of an Earlier People?

According to noted scholar of ancient Mesoamerica Michael E. Smith, some of the Aztecs' gods, including the Feathered Serpent, Quetzalcoatl, and the rain deity Tlaloc, may have originated in the earlier culture centered in the majestic city of Teotihuacan.

the splendors of the past. The Aztec image of the Toltecs was of a people "almost superhuman in their accomplishments," Smith continues. "They were said to have invented most of Mesoamerican culture, including all of the arts and crafts, writing, and the calendar."[7]

Tale of the Toltecs' Demise

In truth, those cultural aspects had existed in the region long before the Toltecs came on the scene, likely having been introduced by the Olmecs. But the Aztecs did not know that, so they idolized the Toltecs and modeled many of their customs on Toltec ones. The Aztecs also felt great sympathy for that earlier people because of the terrible manner in which they had supposedly met their demise.

That sad fate was described in detail in one of the main Aztec myths about the Toltecs. It began with the dark, menacing, and deceptive war god Tezcatlipoca arriving in Tollan disguised as a poor merchant. His body was painted bright green, which made him look extremely strange. Having made most people who saw him uneasy, he next used his godly powers to cause the local king's daughter to fall in love with him. That disturbed not only the king but most of his subjects as well, because all feared the princess might end up marrying the mysterious, creepy stranger.

Hoping to get rid of the merchant, the king ordered him to join the Toltec soldiers who would be stationed in the front line in an upcoming battle with an enemy army. Everyone expected the green-colored oddball to die in the battle. But he surprised them by killing many opposing fighters and thereby emerging as a military hero.

Having enjoyed his game of fooling the Toltecs, the mean-spirited god decided it was time to spring his trap. To celebrate his military deeds as the merchant, the still-disguised

The dark god Tezcatlipoca arrived in Tollan disguised as a poor merchant. Legend says he turned the Toltecs into rocks.

Tezcatlipoca announced that he would hold "a great feast in Tollan, to which all the people for miles around were invited," according to the late mythologist Lewis Spence.

> Great crowds assembled, and danced and sang in the city to the sound of the drum. Tezcatlipoca sang to them and forced them to accompany the rhythm of his song with their feet. Faster and faster the people danced, until the pace became so furious that they were driven to madness, lost their footing, and tumbled pell-mell down a deep ravine, where they were changed into rocks.[8]

The Grand Bargain

This vivid and scary tale taught the Aztecs more than how their admirable predecessors, the Toltecs, had died. It also made it crystal clear that humans, including themselves, were mere playthings to the gods and that those divine beings could wipe out an entire civilization anytime they saw fit. So people must do everything in their power to appease the gods in order to stay on their good side and thereby survive.

The Aztecs took this concept a step further by doing their utmost to impress, as well as appease, the deities they worshipped. One way to do this was to excel at war, conquer other nations, and build an empire, which the Aztecs did with uncanny skill. Another way to impress the gods was to be industrious and create wondrous and everlasting artifacts of their civilization. Like the Teotihuacanos and Toltecs before them, therefore, the Aztecs built an urban center on a grand scale—the splendid Tenochtitlan.

In a similar vein, the Aztecs created extremely large-scale food-production facilities—big raised gardens called *chinampas* that rested in reclaimed swamps. Each garden was closely attended by farmers and other workers who planted seeds and fertilized them with soil enriched with manure made from human wastes collected from Tenochtitlan's latrines (toilets). Together, the *chinampas* and a network of traditional farms located beyond the lake's shores produced huge amounts of the Aztecs' staple foods, maize

Myths About Mictlan

In one of the Aztec creation myths, after crafting the world, the gods in charge of that task deposited the scary-looking deity, Mictlantecuhtli, and his equally hideous wife, Mictecacihuatl, in a gloomy underworld called Mictlan. In this and other myths, Mictlantecuhtli was described as bony, like a skeleton, with blood dripping down his chest and arms. Supposedly, he frequently kept his eyes closed because he had the ability to see without the benefit of eyes. He was fas-cinated by eyes, however, and was said to wear a necklace strung with human eyeballs. Mictlantecuhtli and Mictecaci-huatl shared a windowless castle with droves of bats, owls, and spiders, so the two gruesome deities became associated with those and other creatures that thrive in the dark. The Aztecs believed that Mictlantecuhtli played a major role in their world by separating the souls of dead people into groups, each bound for a different kind of afterlife.

The Lord of the Dead, Mictlantecuhtli, was an ugly god who ruled the gloomy underworld of Mictlan.

Crops Shipped Swiftly in Boats

Scholar David Carrasco explains that the Aztecs built many of their *chinampas* directly on the surface of Texcoco. That allowed workers to load crops into large canoes and swiftly paddle them directly to waiting marketplaces in the island city of Tenochtitlan.

(a kind of corn), beans, squash, and various kinds of fruit. The food supply was usually very stable, which regularly kept the large population of Tenochtitlan and other Aztec towns well fed. The kings and other top leaders were thankful. They were well aware of a reality of all empires in all ages—namely, subjects with full stomachs are less likely to rebel.

Yet this practical aspect of large-scale food production was always quietly overshadowed by the religious need to respect what the gods had done for humans in the past. Based on one of their myths, the Aztecs believed it was neither luck nor human ingenuity that had revealed the secrets of agriculture to people in the first place. Instead, Quetzalcoatl and the sun god Nanahuatzin, aided by some other deities, had expended great effort and determination to find a suitable food source for humanity.

Long ago, the myth begins, the gods had fashioned humans but were disturbed to see there was nothing for these new, fragile little beings to eat. Several of the divinities immediately set out to find food, including the resourceful god of the winds, Quetzalcoatl. After days of searching, he suddenly noticed a tiny red ant carrying a kernel of maize. When questioned, the ant refused to reveal where he had found it, so as the insect continued on its way, the god secretly followed it.

The ant eventually led Quetzalcoatl to a large mountain and crawled out of sight into a crack in its base. Desiring to know what was inside, the god transformed himself into an ant and crawled into the same crack. Inside the mountain, Quetzalcoatl was astounded to find tremendous stores of maize, grains, and seeds. He collected samples of them all and hurried back to his fellow deities. They all agreed that these were the nutritious foods that humans needed to survive, but first they had to be extracted from the mountain that held them. However, even the muscular Quetzalcoatl was not strong enough to break through the massive layers of stone. Finally, however, Nanahuatzin saved the day. As the sun god, he had vast amounts of energy at his disposal, and he blasted through the mountain's side, releasing the billions of trapped seeds and maize kernels.

Thanks to the gods, therefore, humans—including the Aztecs—had all the food they needed, and it was only right to repay those deities with regular worship. As Mexican scholar Guilhem Olivier says, a sort of grand bargain developed between humanity and the divine. He explains:

> The gods provide humans with life, sustenance, and cultural benefits, in exchange for prayers, songs, offerings and sacrifices. This central dependence on divine beings translated into expressions of devotion on the part of the indigenous population that left the Spanish friars in utter awe. Clearly the ancient Mexicans gave frequent expression to a profound veneration of their gods.[9]

Connections with the Gods

None of the Aztecs, no matter how rich and powerful or how poor and powerless, lacked this deep admiration for the gods, and members of all social classes eagerly worshipped those deities in one way or another. For example, at the pinnacle of the social pyramid sat the king, called the *tlatoani* in the Aztecs' language of Nahuatl. He ruled in the name of and vigorously promoted the worship of Huitzilopochtli, the Mexica's national god and a fierce deity of war and human sacrifice.

The monarch reached the throne through an election by a small group of nobles. In certain myths, the gods had ordained that the nobility should enjoy special privileges denied to members of the lower classes. To some degree, therefore, the Aztec nobles owed their high positions to the gods and felt bound in service to them. No less devoted to the divine beings were members of the numerically largest social class—the *macehualtin*, or "commoners." Like other Aztecs, they grew up believing that the gods had established the human social order and that it was their duty to accept their positions in that order.

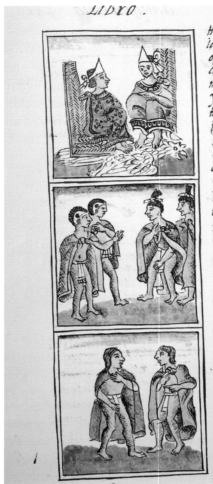

This facsimile from the Codex Florentine, which contains the writings of Friar Bernardino de Sahagun on the Aztecs, shows Aztec nobles. These nobles believed that they owed their high positions to the gods and so felt bound in service to them.

Even members of the lowest social class, the slaves, or *tlacotin*, felt a connection with and obligation to the gods. Aztec slaves were a mix of criminals in servitude as a punishment, war captives, and free persons who temporarily entered slavery to pay off debts. Most slaves were well treated and had multiple paths to gain their freedom, including buying it. In part, this was because myths said the gods recognized them as human beings with an inherent worth and certain basic rights. The shadowy war god Tezcatlipoca, who had destroyed the Toltecs, was said to look on slaves as his own children. He supposedly wanted to protect them from ill treatment by abusive masters. So, like the members of other classes, slaves felt they had good reason to revere and worship the gods.

As in European faiths, including Christianity, that worship consisted of set rituals, including sacrifice, prayer, and taking part in religious festivals honoring the deities. There was a difference, however, in how the Aztecs (and other Mesoamerican peoples) pictured the divinities they honored in those rituals. Whether multiple or single, the gods of the Greeks, Romans, Christians, and most other Europeans were seen to have very human physical attributes. Indeed, "we tend to think of ancient gods in terms of the Greek pantheon," Smith says. "Zeus, Athena, Poseidon, and the other Greek gods were very humanlike, with their own unique personalities, powers, and domains. They often took human form and entered society undetected. Aztec gods, on the other hand, are better viewed as invisible spirits or forces whose roles, natures, and forms blended together."[10] Harvard University scholar David Carrasco agrees and adds:

> All of life was considered inherently sacred and literally filled with the potency of divine beings. The gods were expressions of the sacred powers that permeated the world. . . . To the Aztecs, *teotl* [the word for a god] signified a sacred power manifested in natural forms, such as a tree, a mountain, or a rainstorm, [or] in mysterious and chaotic places, such as caves, whirlpools, or storms.[11]

The Sacred Lake

Thus, the Aztecs felt that there was a very strong connection between people and the natural world around them. Moreover, the gods not only provided that connection to the landscape, they *were* that connection, and as a result, it was believed that many features of the countryside were sacred. These hallowed natural forms included some of those Carrasco mentions, like mountains, caves, and storms. Especially revered and blessed were water forms like rain, lakes, and rivers.

One way the Aztecs translated these concepts into daily worship was to make the most sacred features of the natural world the central focus of daily life. An outstanding example of this approach was the choice of location for the Aztec capital, Tenochtitlan. That magnificent city was erected in the middle of Lake Texcoco not because of the lovely scenic views, but because the huge lake was one of the holiest spots in all of Mesoamerica. It was therefore seen as a place where humans could be close to the gods they so earnestly revered.

In fact, it was the Aztecs' own national god, Huitzilopochtli, who, in a story told in a major myth, led their ancestors to the lake's shore and pointed out the best place to build the city. A separate myth picked up where the first left off and told how the early Aztecs erected their largest and most important religious shrine, the Templo Mayor, in a spot that deity had chosen for them. Like other Mesoamerican peoples, the Aztecs often built their temples atop big stone pyramids. In keeping with their beliefs about the sanctity of natural formations, these pyramids were intended to represent sacred mountains.

But more specifically, as the myth explained, the Templo Mayor (consisting of both the pyramid and the two temples it held up) was meant to mimic the Hill of Coatepec, where Huitzilopochtli himself had been born. In an event strikingly similar to Athena's birth in the famous ancient Greek myth, the mighty Huitzilopochtli emerged from his mother's body as an adult and in a full array of armor. This was necessary because his sister was on her way to kill both him and their mother. A long, bloody battle ensued on the hill's summit, and fortunately for Huitzilopochtli and his mother, he was the victor. After slaying his sister, he cut her body into pieces and tossed them down to the foot of the hill. Accordingly, many centuries later, when the Aztecs built the Templo Mayor, they installed a special stone disk that represented her mutilated corpse at the bottom of the pyramid.

A Graphic Visual Reminder

The importance of this myth to the Aztecs is demonstrated by the fact that in one of their sacred ceremonies they reenacted part of the mythical fight between Huitzilopochtli and his sister. Using the great temple-topped pyramid to stand in for the Hill of Coatepec, priests led a group of warriors to the

top. Often these men who were to be sacrificed in the ritual, called the "victims," were foreign-born war captives, but in some cases they were members of the Aztec community.

When the participants in the ritual reached the summit of the Templo Mayor, the victims danced, presumably to entertain the gods. Then the priests sliced off their heads and hurled the victims down the pyramid's steps, thereby imitating what Huitzilopochtli had done with his sister's body in the myth. This ceremony gave the thousands of Aztec citizens who watched it a graphic visual reminder of the importance of honoring the great god who had made their city in the lake—along with their lives and fortunes—possible.

The victims were not so fortunate, of course. However, it is fascinating to note that they were not always forced to take part. Incredibly by today's standards, sometimes they were willing participants. This was because first, they were devoutly religious, and second, they knew that volunteering would "elevate them to the highly honored status of sacred victim, the status that all warriors strove to attain," according to researcher Lora

A Spanish engraving depicts the Aztec capital of Tenochtitlan at the time of the Spanish conquest.

"The Whole Place Stank!"

Templo Mayor, or "great temple," was the Spanish name for the largest structure in the Aztec capital of Tenochtitlan. The natives' own name for it was the Huey Teocalli, meaning "great god house." It was a massive four-sided pyramid with wide stairways of 114 steps leading up to two temples that stood side by side at the summit. One, painted red, was dedicated to the Aztecs' national god, Huitzilopochtli; the other shrine, colored blue, honored Tlaloc, the rain god. Not surprisingly, Cortés and the other Christian Spaniards who beheld the structure were disturbed that it honored "heathen" gods, not to mention its regular use in human sacrifice. "I always called it that building Hell," one of the Spaniards, Bernal Diaz del Castillo, later wrote. About the statue of Huitzilopochtli at the top, Diaz said, "He had a very broad face and huge, terrible eyes. And there were so many precious stones, so much gold, so many pearls [sticking] to him [that] his whole body and head were covered with them. He was girdled with huge snakes made of gold and precious stones, and in one hand he held a bow, in the other some arrows." Diaz added with disgust, "All the walls of that shrine were so splashed and caked with blood that they and the floor were black. Indeed, the whole place stank!"

Bernal Diaz del Castillo. *The Conquest of New Spain*. Translated by J.M. Cohen. New York: Penguin, 1963, p. 236.

The ruins of the Templo Mayor, or "great temple," can still be seen in present day Mexico City.

L. Kile. "Looking at sacrifice from the Aztec perspective," the act of "shedding one's blood or giving one's life" to appease the national god "was the ultimate gift one could make to the community."[12] Perhaps better than any other single example, this shows the tremendous power of religion, including its built-in myths, on ancient Aztec society and life.

CHAPTER 2

Life Out of Death: The Creation of the World

It has been established that the Aztecs were strongly preoccupied with tales about the beginnings of things—for instance, how maize and other grains and seeds became people's staple foods, how the site of Tenochtitlan was chosen, and how the Aztec national god Huitzilopochtli was born as an adult warrior. It is only natural then, that Aztec mythology should contain stories about how the cosmos (universe) and the gods themselves came to be. In fact, the Aztecs' creation tales are among their most complex and colorful myths.

Duality in the Natural Order

At the same time, an examination of the Aztecs' myths as a whole shows that they were no less concerned with endings and death than with births and beginnings. That concern was with the downfalls not only of individual people, but of entire civilizations as well. One clear example is the tale of Tezcatlipoca's wanton destruction of the Toltecs. This compelling, sometimes morbid interest in the ultimate demise of peoples and nations was almost certainly inspired by the sight of so many ruined, abandoned cities in central Mexico. From their existence, the Aztecs concluded that all civilizations are transient, or temporary, and that they all fade away and vanish sooner or later.

Yet the majestic remnants of those fallen cultures also injected a note of optimism in the Aztec worldview. True, human civilizations tend to pass away over time, that note seemed to suggest. Yet new ones seem always to rise upon their wreckage and flourish in their individual moments in

The Aztec national god, Huitzilopochtli, was believed to be a deity representing both life and death.

the sun. In this way the Aztecs came to believe that as a matter of course life, or creation, springs out of death, and civilizations rise and fall in a cyclic manner. There is, therefore, a trade-off, or duality—a balance between opposites—built into the natural order, according to the Aztecs' view of the cosmos. Take heart, it told them, for though death is inevitable, the pain and sorrow it brings are just as certainly offset by life's renewal, or new creation. The Aztecs saw this balance between death and renewal all around them.

One of the more glaring examples was the nature of their patron god, Huitzilopochtli. On the one hand, he was a deity of war and death, and on the other he was the mighty sun god. (Nanahuatzin, who cracked open the mountain containing the first maize and seeds, was not the only sun god. The Aztecs believed that more than half a dozen deities acted as sun gods over time, the most recent being Huitzilopochtli.) In the guise of the sun, Huitzilopochtli brought the warmth that was required to grow crops, so he made agriculture, with its constant renewal of plant life, possible. Inevitably, all plants died, yet new ones were destined to grow in their place in the following year's growing season. So Huitzilopochtli contained within him the duality of death and life, or creation, one giving way to the other in an eternal pattern.

A similar obsession with the dual concepts of death and life can be seen in the Aztecs' annual agricultural festival, says noted researcher Norman Bancroft Hunt. That celebration "marked the first shoots of the young maize bursting from the seed," he adds. The deity honored—Xipe Totec, a creator god and the bringer of spring rains—was widely known as the Flayed Lord. The word *flayed* means "lashed" or "skinned." As Hunt explains, the name came from the god's

> association with the maize bursting its skin, since at the height of the ritual a sacrificial captive was flayed alive and his skin donned either by the warrior who had captured him or the priest conducting the ceremony. The skin was sewn in place and worn until it rotted and the bindings burst open in a symbolic reenactment of the bursting of the seed. But this also symbolized the necessity of death and burial—as the maize seed dies and is buried—so that renewal of life is possible.[13]

Nata, Nena, and Noah

The Aztecs had a myth that closely paralleled the biblical story of Noah, the great flood, and the ark. Not long before the end of the fourth age, the Aztec version went, the god Tezcatlipoca warned a human couple that a terrible flood would soon come. The man and wife, Nata and Nena (in some versions, Coxcox and Xochiquetzal), were told to build a boat from the trunk of a cypress tree and to bring along an ear of maize for each of them. They should eat nothing else but the maize, the god warned. The two people did as the deity instructed. They fashioned a vessel, and after the predicted deluge came, they watched as the world was flooded and the rest of the humans turned into fish. After the disaster was at last over, Nata and Nena's boat floated through the waters for several days, during which they ate the maize they had taken along. Growing hungry, they caught some fish and wolfed them down. Tezcatlipoca, the great Smoking Mirror, saw this, hurried to them, and shouted that they had disobeyed his order to eat only the maize. The fearful Nata and Nena apologized profusely, but it was no use. The vengeful, dark-hearted god immediately turned them into dogs.

A Dual Personality

These themes—duality in nature, death and renewal, and the repeated creation of life and civilizations from the remnants of dead things—permeate all of the Aztecs' creation myths. The concept of duality, for example, is immediately apparent in the story of the creation of the cosmos, or world. The original and most powerful god of creation, Ometeotl, had a dual personality. Also a deity of fire and light, "he" displayed both male and female traits, as emphasized in an ancient Aztec song. "He is the Lord and Lady of Duality," it begins.

> He is Lord and Lady of our maintenance. He is mother and father of the gods, the old god. He is at the same time the god of fire who dwells in the navel of fire. He is the mirror of day and night. He is the star which illumines all things and he is the Lady of the shining skirt of stars. He is our mother, our father. Above all, he is Ometeotl, who dwells in the place of duality, Omeyocan [the highest level of Heaven].[14]

One of the most striking aspects of Ometeotl's physical duality was that, being both male and female, he could mate with himself. According to the myth, that is exactly what he did—and in the process, he set the creation in motion. In this way the great primeval god, who in the words of one major scholar possessed "the cosmic energy upon which everything depended,"[15] was able to produce four divine sons. From the eldest to the youngest, they were Xipe Totec, Tezcatlipoca, Quetzalcoatl, and Huitzilopochtli.

It is only natural to ask how Ometeotl could have given rise to Huitzilopochtli. After all, there was another myth that described how Huitzilopochtli had emerged from the body of a goddess who had already birthed his sister, whom he killed soon after his own birth. The explanation for this seeming contradiction demonstrates how the Aztecs subtly manipulated their creation myths to suit their needs and circumstances.

First, most of the peoples who dwelled in central Mexico before the Aztecs' arrival recognized the creation story involving Ometeotl, which the Aztecs adopted when they entered the region. Second, prior to that entry, Huitzilopochtli was not the youngest of the four offspring of the original creator god Ometeotl. That youngest deity's name was Maquizoatl. After the Aztecs migrated to central Mexico from somewhere to the north, they were bothered by the fact that the region's principal creation myth did not mention their patron deity, Huitzilopochtli. So they substituted him for Maquizoatl in the tale, thereby raising their national god to the same level of importance as Tezcatlipoca and Quetzalcoatl. Third, a by-product of that reworking of the myth was that two versions of Huitzilopochtli's birth now existed—one, involving his mother, which the Aztecs brought with them to central Mexico, and the one that had originally belonged to Maquizoatl.

The Aztecs recognized and celebrated both of these birth stories. There was no contradiction here, in their eyes, because in their religion and mythology even the gods could die and be reborn. That meant that any god could potentially have multiple birth stories.

The Initial Round of Creation

Returning to the birth story in which Ometeotl produced offspring, the Aztecs and other peoples in the region associated those four young gods with colors. Xipe Totec was red, Tezcatlipoca was black, Quetzalcoatl was white, and Huitzilopochtli was blue. They also stood for the four cardinal directions, or points—East for Xipe Totec, North for Tezcatlipoca, West for Quetzalcoatl, and South for Huitzilopochtli.

Once they sorted out who stood for what, these recently created divinities proceeded to do some creating of their

A page from the Codex Fejérváry-Mayer shows Ometeotl, the fire god, at the center of the universe being fed on the blood of sacrifice, which flows from the head, hands, legs, and ribs of the dark god Tezcatlipoca.

A Real Case of Foot in Mouth

The giant sea monster Cipactli in the Aztec creation myth was said to have an insatiable appetite. In fact, he had many mouths, including one located at each joint in his body. One of these mouths devoured one of the god Tezcatlipoca's feet during the battle in which the creator deities defeated Cipactli.

own. They fashioned the oceans, and within one they tinkered together a gigantic sea monster called Cipactli. Then they attacked the creature and tore it apart by pulling from the four directions they symbolized. One section of Cipactli became the heavens, of which there were thirteen levels; another of the monster's parts was transformed into the wide, flat disk of earth, with its mountains, valleys, and lakes.

The Aztecs called this huge combination of landscape and seascape Cemanahuac, which means "the land surrounded by water." The name accurately reflects the fact that the physical world the Aztecs and their neighbors knew—Mexico—was tucked between two oceans, one in the east, the other in the west. People envisioned that these vast waterways stretched away from the land for many miles and eventually rose up into wall-like liquid pillars that helped hold up the sky. This mythical view of the seas apparently kept the Aztecs from imagining the existence of other vast lands lying on those waterways' far sides. That partially explains their surprise when the Spaniards arrived and said that they were from a nation located on the other end of the Aztecs' eastern ocean.

Ometeotl's sons also created Mictlan, the shadowy realm of the dead, from Cipactli's huge dismembered tail. Clearly, someone had to be in charge of that unwelcome place, so the creators made two gods to fulfill that role—the skeleton-like Mictlantecuhtli and his equally scary-looking wife, Mictecacihuatl. The creation of other gods followed, among them the rain god Tlaloc; his first wife, Xochiquetzal, goddess of flowers, corn, and sex; and his second wife (or in some stories his sister), Chalchiuhtlicue, who watched over lakes, seas, and rivers. The creator gods also manufactured the days and months and even time itself. In addition, they ingeniously invented the calendar to keep track of the passage of those time periods.

The First Four Suns

Near the end of this enormous, well-ordered surge of creation, trouble set in, as Ometeotl's four resourceful offspring began to quarrel. Their main disagreement was over the sun. Clearly, the world could not be considered complete and whole without a bright sun to provide the energy needed to grow crops and the warmth required to keep life from freezing to death. The question was: Which of the many recently created gods would become the sun god and in that role rule the world?

Unfortunately for all concerned, the answer to this query was a huge battle for supremacy that took place over a series of centuries-long ages appropriately called "Suns." As a noted expert on the Aztecs, Miguel Leon-Portilla, summarizes it, each of several different gods "endeavored to identify himself with the sun." This was so he could "direct the destiny of the world. During each age, or Sun, of the earth, one god prevailed over the others." Inevitably, however, "at the end of each age, war broke out and destruction followed."[16] Overall, it turned out, most of the bickering was between Quetzalcoatl and Tezcatlipoca, as each either became the sun god or else assigned some other deity to play that role.

In the first age, called the Jaguar Sun, Tezcatlipoca ruled the world, then populated by human-like giants who lived by eating acorns. For a few centuries, all seemed fine. But then Quetzalcoatl snuck up on his enemy Tezcatlipoca and knocked him out of the sky, after which the fallen god got revenge by sending jaguars to devour the giants. So the first age ended in a bloodbath.

The second age was known as the Wind Sun. This time Quetzalcoatl assumed the role of sun god, and he reigned over a race of normal-size human-like beings who subsisted on nuts. After a few centuries had elapsed, the still fuming Tezcatlipoca caused trouble by turning the nut eaters into monkeys. Furious, Quetzalcoatl summoned up powerful hurricanes to blow away the monkeys, thereby ending that age.

For the third age, Quetzalcoatl convinced Tlaloc to be the sun god. Tlaloc ruled another race of early humans who ate

A bas-relief of Quetzalcoatl, who in the second age assumed the role of sun god and reigned over a race of human-like beings who subsisted on nuts.

water lilies, and at first it appeared that the world would be stable and long lasting. But that was not to be, because still again Tezcatlipoca instigated misery, this time by seducing and stealing away Tlaloc's wife Xochiquetzal. Tlaloc was so upset that he refused to allow rain to fall, causing a terrible drought. He eventually destroyed the world in a different kind of rain—a shower of fire.

Next, Quetzalcoatl initiated the fourth age—the Water Sun—by assigning Tlaloc's second spouse, Chalchiuhtlicue, the role of sun goddess. Her reign was mostly unhappy because the mean-spirited Tezcatlipoca denounced her and eventually knocked her out of the sky. When he did this, part of the sky broke open, releasing immense quantities of water that fell to earth and created a great flood. The people then alive would have drowned if not for some gods who changed them into fish at the last minute.

Dawn of the Fifth Sun

The Aztecs who built Tenochtitlan, carved out an empire, and suffered defeat at the hands of Cortés believed that they lived in the fifth age. They gave that one, which supposedly is still ongoing today, the name of Earthquake Sun. This was based on the Aztecs' fascination with repeated cycles of creation and destruction. The fact that the first four ages had ended in catastrophe made them assume that the fifth one would also end badly. Indeed, they were convinced that at some time in the future, massive earthquakes would topple the mountains and that monsters sent by the gods would devour the few humans who managed to survive the quakes.

More importantly, one of the Aztecs' principal and most memorable religious customs was based directly on a series of events they believed occurred at the start of the fifth age. When the floodwaters that had destroyed the fourth age receded, the story goes, earth's land surfaces were devoid of life and the sunless world was dark and bleak. The worried gods all gathered near the Pyramid of the Sun, in the giant plaza at Teotihuacan. That choice of meeting place was intended to symbolize their desire to once more cause a bright, warm sun to move across the sky each day.

After much discussion, the deities decided that a new and hopefully longer-lasting human race should be created.

But first, a sun must be fashioned for them, and it must be more stable and reliable than those in the past. To ensure that the forthcoming humans would have a dependable sun, the gods decided that some of them must sacrifice their own lives. By jumping into a huge and very hot fire, they would die and be transformed into a brilliant, sizzling sun. According to Bernardino de Sahagun, a Spanish priest who lived among the Aztecs after Cortés conquered them, one deity called out:

> "Come hither. O gods! Who will carry the burden? Who will take it upon himself to be the sun, to bring the dawn?" And upon this, one of them who was there spoke. Tecuciztecatl [deity of seashells] presented himself. He said: "O Gods, I will be the one." And again the gods spoke: "And who else?" Whereupon, they looked around at one another. They pondered the matter. They said to one another, "How may this be? How may we decide?" No one dared. No one else came forward. Everyone was afraid. They all drew back. There was present, however, a god named Nanauatzin [who oversaw skin diseases], [and] as he stood listening, the gods called to him and said, "You shall be the one." He eagerly accepted the decision, saying, "It is well, O gods. You have been good to me."[17]

The two divinities stepped up to edge of a raging fire built in front of the Pyramid of the Sun, and contemplating the searing pain he was about to feel, Tecuciztecatl hesitated. But then Nanauatzin gathered his own courage and leaped in. Seeing this, Tecuciztecatl shed his caution and quickly followed. After this, Sahagun continues,

> when both had cast themselves into the flames, when they had already burned, then the gods sat waiting to see where Nanauatzin would come to rise—he who fell first into the fire—in order that he might shine [as the sun], in order that the dawn might break. . . . And when the sun came to rise, when he burst forth . . . it was impossible to look into his face. He blinded one with his light. Intensely did he shine![18]

Priests and Priestesses: "A Terrible Picture"

The colorful public religious ceremonies the Aztecs held numerous times each year were conducted by members of the nation's priesthood. Most were men, although a few priestesses also took part. Whether male or female, these religious personnel started their training as children by going to a *calmecac*, a special school that only members of the noble class were allowed to attend. There they learned about the gods, the myths associated with them, the beliefs and rituals of the Aztec religion, and the duties they would perform when they became full-fledged priests or priestesses. Among those duties were conducting the sacrifices, or offerings, to the gods; maintaining the sacred fires in the temples; and playing drums, flutes, and other musical instruments during the rituals. In some of these ceremonies, priests and priestesses were stained by smoke from burning wood and incense, blood from human victims, and/or some of their own blood, spilled when they pierced their own ears, tongues, and lips as part of rituals. "Priests must have presented a terrible picture to outsiders," says historian Michael E. Smith. "Their faces and bodies were dyed black. Much of their body was scarred and mutilated from constant bloodletting. Their unwashed hair, worn long, became matted with dried blood."

Michael E. Smith. *The Aztecs*. Oxford, England: Blackwell, 2002, p. 221.

Aztec priests perform a ritual human sacrifice.

The gods Tecuciztecatl and Nanauatzin leaped into a fire in front of the Pyramid of the Sun (shown here in background) and became two suns.

Repaying an Enormous Debt

Tecuciztecatl also rose up, becoming a second brilliant sky disk. But two suns made it too hard for anyone to see. So one of the deities threw a rabbit at Tecuciztecatl, thereby dimming his light, and thereafter he became the moon. (The Aztecs claimed they could see the outline of a rabbit on the moon's face.)

As thrilled as they were by the sun's creation, the gods now beheld a new dilemma. Once that shining orb had risen high in the sky, it no longer moved, which meant that the days would no longer pass and time would stand still. The deities, in their wisdom, realized that there was only one solution to this problem. They all had to follow Tecuciztecatl's and Nanauatzin's example. They must all sacrifice themselves for the good of the future humans by jumping into the fire, which would give the sun the momentum it needed to move. So in a true display of heroism, the gods lined up. Quetzalcoatl then cut out their hearts one by one, including his own, and tossed them into the flames, after which they all leaped in. (Although those deities could feel pain and die, they had the power to be reborn and return to the cosmos, which they did a while later.)

To the Aztecs, the myth of the fifth age and the creation of the sun was not simply a quaint, at times moving story of the gods' courage. This story inspired the Aztecs so much that they incorporated it into their real-life religious practices. In particular, it became the ideological basis of their custom of human sacrifice. In simple terms, says Michael E. Smith, "just as these gods sacrificed themselves for the sun, so too people had to provide blood and hearts to keep the sun going."[19] Thus, since the gods had willingly given their own lives to guarantee humanity's ongoing survival, people owed them an enormous debt. What is more, it was only right that humans should repay that debt by acting in a like manner and providing blood sacrifices.

Cortés and his soldiers actually witnessed some of these human sacrifices, which they viewed as barbaric; while in contrast, the Aztecs saw them as sacred and perfectly civilized. According to the Spanish accounts, specially trained priests called "fire sellers" used flint knives to cut the hearts from the sacrificial victims. In the words of Spaniard Bernal Diaz del Castillo, the priests "sawed open their chests and drew out their palpitating hearts and offered them to the idols [statues] that were there, and they kicked the bodies down the steps [of the pyramid]."[20]

Myths as Memories

It must also be noted that Aztecs believed this gory repayment of the debt they owed their gods had to happen on a regular basis, year after year. Otherwise, the world would be destroyed by catastrophe well before the prophesied earthquakes came. Whether it was earthquakes, fires, floods, or other disasters that ended the cyclic historical ages, the Aztecs clearly did not pick these calamities randomly. Nor were these events figments of their imaginations. Modern historians think they and other Mesoamericans possessed assorted recollections of real disasters that had passed down orally—that is, by word of mouth—over the generations. The late scholar and mythologist Carleton Beals suggested these were "race memories of early catastrophes that wiped out whole peoples—floods, hurricanes, earthquakes, and volcanic eruptions. Perhaps one of these myths reflects the great downpour of fire and lava that long ago swept away the folk of the circular wind temple of Cuicuilco, in the southern end of the Valley of Mexico."[21]

Beals here refers to a major volcanic eruption that occurred in the year A.D. 400. At the time, the Cuicuilco temple was the center of a bustling town of some twenty thousand people. When the nearby Xitle volcano blew its top, the town was buried beneath lava and other debris, and memories of the catastrophe no doubt provided fodder for the myths of later peoples, including the Aztecs. Indeed, "No one forgot about Cuicuilco," researcher Philip Coppens writes.

> It became a pilgrimage centre for the refugees and their descendants who came to see the city that the volcano had destroyed. For them, the site must have confirmed several of their "beliefs," for figurines and stelae [stone markers] from Cuicuilco indicate that the inhabitants worshiped the fire god Huehueteotl, which is not surprising since the Xitle volcano was likely active during Cuicuilco's occupation, sporadically rumbling and blowing smoke, and eventually destroying the site.[22]

The Oldest City?

The ancient pyramid at Cuicuilco, where people worshipped the fire god in some Mesoamerican myths, was first excavated in 1917 by Mexican archaeologist Manuel Gamio. He and later experts concluded that the town surrounding it may be the oldest city in the Valley of Mexico.

The Aztecs believed that a similar but even larger disaster might happen in the near or not-too-distant future. This was because they broke time down into fifty-two-year segments and thought that the fifth age—the Earthquake Sun—would end at the close of a fifty-two-year cycle, though they did not know which one. As a result, they celebrated an extremely strange and unique religious festival every fifty-two years. Called the New Fire Festival, it

consisted of very real preparations for the end of the world. People burned everything movable, including all their furniture and other belongings. Then, if the world did *not* end, they started over, dutifully replacing the things they had destroyed. In all the world's mythologies, few examples of a people's myths affecting their everyday lives are as unusual and dramatic as this one.

The destruction of the Cuicuilco Pyramid (pictured) by a volcano in A.D. 400 influenced later Aztec myths of destruction.

CHAPTER 3

Descent into Hell: The Making of Humanity

In addition to their tales about the creation of the world, the Aztecs had myths that explained how the various human races came to be during the five ages, or Suns. The most important of these stories to the average Aztec was the one that told about the creation of his own race at the beginning of the fifth age, or Earthquake Sun. That tale, in which the Feathered Serpent, the great god Quetzalcoatl, was the chief character, was significant from a "historical" standpoint. This was because, as with other ancient peoples and their own myths, the Aztecs believed the myth's events actually occurred. So to them it was a slice of history.

Another reason the story was important was that it educated people about various features of their culture, customs, and beliefs. From it, for example, they learned about the afterlife, including the multiple levels of the underworld called Mictlan, as well as the more pleasant places to which the souls of some individuals went. The tale explained the sources of many of the customs surrounding their religious rituals as well, along with several other aspects of daily life.

A Series of Obstacles

The incidents of the major myth in question are set early in the fifth age. In the dramatic climax of the prior era, the Water

Sun, a huge flood had swept over the land, and people had been transformed into fish. So when the rushing waters finally receded, no humans lived on earth's surface. Meanwhile, before sacrificing themselves in the massive bonfire in Teotihuacan, the gods had expressed their strong desire to make a new, longer-lasting race of humans. So when those deities revived themselves, restored their scorched bodies to normalcy, and returned to earth, they were ready to go forward with that plan.

After discussing the upcoming creation of humans at length, the gods agreed that the versatile and trustworthy creator deity Quetzalcoatl would take charge of the project. As always, he was eager to populate the barren earth with a race of people. But he immediately perceived a major obstacle. Namely, when the past race of humans had turned into fish, their human bones were left behind, and these ended up in the deep, dark subterranean caverns of Mictlan. Quetzalcoatl realized that he needed those bones to properly replenish the human race and that he would have to journey down to the hell-like Mictlan and retrieve them. In order to accomplish that task, the god would have to make it through all of the underworld's nine levels, which had been installed many centuries before by Quetzalcoatl himself and his fellow creators.

By hearing this myth recited when they were young, Aztec children learned that each underworld level contained a physical obstacle that was difficult to traverse. They also learned that when humans died, most of their souls had to pass through at least some, if not all, of these levels, or stages. As noted scholar of ancient Mesoamerica Manuel Aguilar-Moreno explains, "In the first stage the dead had to cross a river called Apanohuaya. At the moment they reached the shore, they required the assistance of the Techichi dog, which had been buried with them, to swim across the river."[23]

The Techichi dogs mentioned in the myth held a prominent place in the lives of large numbers of Aztecs. The Techichi, a small breed similar to the Chihuahua, had been very popular

A Dozen Dogs Found

Not all Aztec dogs were buried with their masters. In early 2014 the remains of a dozen Techichis were unearthed during excavations of a section of ancient Tenochtitlan. The reason they were buried separately, without human companions, is not yet known.

Techichi dogs, similar to this chihuahua, are mentioned in the Aztec myth of creation and held a prominent place in the lives of large numbers of Aztecs.

among the Toltecs, and the Aztecs, who often emulated that earlier people, adopted it, too. Archaeologists have long been aware that it was common for these canines to be buried with their Aztec masters. The belief was that such a dog could help guide a person's soul through the various levels of the underworld and protect that human spirit along the way. These mythological traits were no doubt based on the fact that dogs are loyal and helpful to humans, and also that they have a calming effect that reduces their masters' stress levels and fears.

The Soul's Journey Continues

"After emerging from the river completely naked," Aguilar-Moreno writes, "the next barrier [the souls faced] was to pass between [two] fierce mountains that constantly crashed against each other." After that, the wandering spirits had to climb another mountain that featured a surface covered with razor-sharp pieces of obsidian (a rock composed of volcanic glass). Aguilar-Moreno continues:

> The next trial led the dead to cross eight gorges where freezing temperatures facilitated a never-ending snowfall and eight valleys where brutal winds cut through them like a knife. After surpassing this, they walked down a path that exposed them to a flurry of innumerable arrows, only to discover that a jaguar had eaten their hearts. The next obstruction consisted of passing a mysterious place called "where the flags wave," where the dead would find a type of lizard or crocodile called Xochitonatl.[24]

The last obstacle the dead souls encountered was composed of nine rivers that had to be crossed, after which they finally met Mictlan's bony-headed ruler, Mictlantecuhtli. The entire journey through the eight levels to reach the ninth was thought to take four years. But that in itself presented still another difficulty seen by many as worse than the earlier ones. In a terrible twist of fate, after the passage of four years the human souls forgot where they had come from and lost all memories of their life on earth.

The Aztecs dreaded this loss of identity, so thinking about death, which conjured up the idea of descending through Mictlan, often made people feel fearful and anxious. Because they viewed the afterlife as a place where self-awareness might be lost, many Aztecs had a sense of foreboding about death. Following the Spanish conquest, European missionaries exploited these negative feelings about life after death with considerable success. The more positive vision of the Christian afterlife in heaven was very appealing to many Aztecs and contributed to their decision to adopt Christianity.

Mictlantecuhtli's Ruse

As a divine being, Quetzalcoatl did not have to worry about losing his identity, as mere humans did. Yet as mighty as he was, he did not look forward to descending through the underworld's treacherous layers. He was well aware that even

The last obstacle the souls of the dead encountered was composed of nine rivers that had to be crossed, after which they finally met Mictlan's bony-headed ruler, Mictlantecuhtli.

if he made it through them all, he would then have to face the skull-headed god of that realm, whom he had helped create in the dim past. That subterranean deity was quite powerful and had been known to tear some visitors apart with his enormous claws. What urged Quetzalcoatl onward in the dangerous voyage into hell was the realization that this was the only way to retrieve the bones needed to create a new race of people.

Quetzalcoatl managed to make it to the bottom level of Mictlan in part because he was assisted by his faithful dog, Xolotl. Just as ordinary Aztecs often entered the afterlife with their Techichi dogs at their sides, the Feathered Serpent took along a divine counterpart of those mortal pups. Xolotl was depicted in various ways by Aztec artists. Sometimes he looked like the Mexican hairless dog (given the name Xoloitzcuiatle in his honor by modern zoologists) that was common, along with the Techichi, in the region. Other Aztec images of Xolotl showed him as Quetzalcoatl's twin, only with a dog's head, and still others depicted him as a skeleton or monstrous animal with his feet pointing backward. In whatever ways the Aztecs pictured him, Quetzalcoatl's canine companion helped him cross rivers and climb mountains during the arduous journey through the stages of Mictlan.

Quetzalcoatl's faithful dog Xolotl was depicted in various ways by Aztec artists. This is a copy of one by a sixteenth-century sculptor.

Having made it through those layers of the underworld, Quetzalcoatl at last came face-to-face with the bony master of that nether realm. Mictlantecuhtli gave the divine visitor a suspicious look and asked what he wanted. "I come in search of the precious bones in your possession," Quetzalcoatl answered. The lord of Mictlan then inquired, "What shall you do with them, Quetzalcoatl?" The latter gave the honest reply, "The gods are anxious that someone should inhabit the earth." Mictlantecuhtli paused and paced back and forth, clearly giving the matter some serious thought. Finally, he said, "Very well. Sound my shell horn and go around my circular realm four times."[25] If the Feathered Serpent did those things, the other god promised, he would be allowed to take the bones back to earth.

But this was lie. Mictlantecuhtli did not want Quetzalcoatl to take the bones, so he conjured up a ruse. The shell horn had no holes, which meant that the god of the winds would not be able to play it and would thereby fail the test Mictlantecuhtli had proposed. The clever Quetzalcoatl managed to solve this problem, however, by ordering some worms to drill holes in the shell and asking some bees to cause the horn to vibrate and emit sound. Hearing the horn play, Mictlantecuhtli had no choice but to let his opponent gather up the bones.

But the ruler of Mictlan did not give up on stopping Quetzalcoatl. Mictlantecuhtli had some of his helpers dig a deep pit in the path that the other god would soon tread on his way out of the ninth level. Sure enough, Quetzalcoatl fell in the pit and dropped the bones, some of which broke and were gnawed by flocks of quail. But the valiant Quetzalcoatl was undaunted. He leaped up, gathered the bones once more, and escaped.

Bones and Blood Combined

On his way back to earth, Quetzalcoatl passed through Tamoanchan, a place the Aztecs thought of as a kind of paradise where gods often roamed through tranquil forests and flower-carpeted meadows. There he sought out the aged mother goddess Cihuaoatl. She was a bringer of

The Aztecs and Man's Best Friend

The Aztecs enjoyed a strong and happy relationship with dogs, today often called "man's best friend." In Tenochtitlan and other Aztec towns, dogs acted as people's companions and protectors as they do today. Researcher Renee McGarry of the online site Mexicolore, a treasure trove of accurate knowledge about Aztec civilization, provides more detail:

Early Spanish visitors to the American continent noted four different kinds of dogs living among the Aztecs, and three of these were domesticated. The fourth type of dog, labeled the *itzcuintepoztli* in Nahuatl, the language of the Aztecs, was a wild dog that some Spanish chroniclers called "the Eater." . . . The village dogs were companions to the Aztecs, and some were identified as the *xoloitzcuintle* (*xolo*), or the Mexican hairless dog. These dogs were rare and valued throughout the empire. . . . *Xolos* are still around today, and their appearance hasn't changed that much since Aztec times. Their hairlessness is caused by a genetic mutation, and puppies born in any litter can have a variety of amounts of hair. (You even see some with just a tuft of hair on their head! I always thought this was groomed, but it can sometimes be natural.) *Xolos* ranged greatly in size, weighing anywhere from ten to fifty pounds, with sleek and muscular bodies. The dogs came in many colors, most commonly in black, blue, and red. They had long, slim necks and almond-shaped eyes, with large ears.

Renee McGarry. "Dog." Mexicolore. www.mexicolore .co.uk/aztecs/flora-and-fauna/dog.

fertility, especially when helping women become pregnant. In a related vein, she protected midwives and women who died in childbirth.

As was so often the case with Aztec myths, people incorporated beliefs and customs from Cihuaoatl's story into their daily lives. She was frequently portrayed in art carrying a spear and shield, like a warrior. This reflected the Aztec conviction that during childbirth a woman underwent a heroic ordeal equal to that of a warrior fighting for his life in battle. Women who died in childbirth were therefore accorded honors equal to fallen soldiers, while Cihuaoatl protected their souls.

Because Cihuaoatl was so closely associated with birth and midwifery, Quetzalcoatl felt she was the perfect deity to aid him in birthing the new race of humans. She eagerly accepted this honor. As researcher and storyteller Angel Vigil tells it, she

> ground the bones into a fine powder and placed them into a ceremonial bowl. For four nights, the gods prayed over the bones. On the fourth night, the gods stood over the ceremonial bowl and pierced their skin. The blood of the gods mixed with the powdered bones and, in four days, the first man rose out of the bowl. Four days later, the first woman rose out of the bowl. Quetzalcoatl's bold journey to the land of the dead had given the human race another chance for life. The blood of the gods and the bones of human ancestors had combined to create a new race of people to live on the earth.[26]

Giving Thanks for Human Creation

Thus, according to Aztec mythology, humans were in debt to the gods for even more than creating the earth and ensuring there was a warm sun in the sky. People also owed thanks to those divinities for fashioning the human race from their own blood. The chief manner in which the Aztecs expressed those thanks was to stage public religious ceremonies that were, in anthropologist Brian Fagan's words, "elaborate, carefully organized productions." They were "conducted in eye-catching settings intended to impress spectators and to promote loyalty to the gods who stood behind the community, the city, and the state."[27]

It has been established that some Aztec religious ceremonies involved human sacrifice, which people today view as grim and grisly. It has also been pointed out that these bloody rituals were intended to pay the debt humans owed the gods for the sacrifice those deities made to ensure the world would have a sun. Yet not all the Aztecs' religious offerings entailed the ritual killing of people. In fact, most of the sacrifices they conducted in a given year were offerings of plants, flowers, maize and other food-crops, and other types of vegetation, as well as several kinds of animals. As the late, noted scholar of Mesoamerica Eleanor Wake pointed out, these "ritual activities dominated life across most of the year."[28]

Those nonhuman sacrifices were also meant to pay back debts that people owed the gods. But the offerings of animals, flowers, fruits, and so forth gave thanks more for those deities' creation of humans in the paradise of Tamoanchan, along with the ongoing favor the gods showed to people on a yearly and even a daily basis. Appropriately, therefore, the Aztec priests sacrificed hundreds of animals to the gods each and every day. Various creatures were offered, but particularly abundant were birds, including owls, turkeys, herons, ducks, hawks, doves, grouse, and hummingbirds.

Most especially among the birds offered, it appears, were quail. The emphasis on that bird was likely an allusion, or direct reference, to the quail that chewed on the human bones

A page from Diego Duran's 1579 publication The History of the Indies of New Span *chronicles the elaborate and bloody sacrificial ceremonies of the Aztecs.*

after Quetzalcoatl fell into the pit in the myth. In the sacrificial ritual, those birds were killed amid the smoke from pans containing burning incense. (The exact purpose of the incense is unclear, but some scholars think it might have been employed to purify the air in the vicinity of the offering.) The Spanish priest Bernardino de Sahagun, who witnessed these ceremonies firsthand, wrote, "Each day, when the sun arose, quails were slain and incense was offered. And [this is how the] quail [were] slain. They [the priests] wrung the necks of the quail and raised them [up], [and thereby] dedicated them to the sun."[29]

Re-creating Paradise

It was significant to the Aztecs that in the myth of Quetzalcoatl's retrieval of the bones, the new race of humans emerged in Tamoanchan. Like the Christian Spaniards who arrived in 1519, whose religion depicted the creation of humans in the

A mural depicts the Aztec second paradise, Tlalocan, where people who died of certain diseases or lightning strikes went in the afterlife.

Garden of Eden, the Aztecs envisioned that they themselves had first appeared in a similar land of beauty and bliss. In fact, when the Catholic friars who accompanied Hernán Cortés told some Aztecs about the Garden of Eden, the natives remarked that their own faith had a similar kind of paradise where humanity was born.

The Aztecs recognized another mythical paradise called Tlalocan, presided over by the rain god Tlaloc. They told Sahagun that Tlalocan was a land of unsurpassed splendor where there was no pain or hunger. "There is much well-being" in Tlalocan, Sahagun wrote, and "much wealth. There is no suffering. There is no lack of maize, squash . . . tomatoes, string beans, [and] marigolds."[30] According to Aztec mythology and the religious beliefs based on it, the souls of people who died of certain diseases, by drowning, or by a lightning strike ended up in sacred Tlalocan, rather than in the lowest level of Mictlan. Both Tamoanchan and Tlalocan were said to be located in mystical regions that in some accounts floated somewhere below the disk of earth and in others somewhere above it.

Some modern experts think that both of these Aztec paradises were based on a single earlier native version. Some evidence suggests it was seen as a magical celestial realm located along the axis of the cosmos. It was also said to contain a great sacred tree similar to the one containing the forbidden apple eaten by Eve in the first book of the Old Testament.

More importantly, the Aztecs frequently referenced these paradises in their daily lives by designing the visual aspects of their sacrificial religious rituals around them. They pictured those mystical realms as places filled with flowers, lush green foliage, sweetly singing birds with long colorful feathers, and other examples of rich, abundant flora and fauna. Accordingly, Aztec artists re-created these images in their public ceremonies. Appropriately, since these mystical realms were sacred, like mountains, the ceremonies were

Why Are People Tall or Short?

In the Aztec myth of humanity's creation, when Quetzalcoatl fell into the pit while trying to escape Mictlan, he dropped the human bones and some of them broke. The Aztecs believed this explained why people come in different sizes!

staged on or around the Aztecs' artificial sacred mountains—the temple-topped pyramids.

The sacrificial ceremonies that captured slices of paradise were nothing less than "magnificent," Wake wrote. Typical features included colorful processions (solemn religious parades); music that followed "the incessant beating of drums"; the ornate costumes of Aztec warriors; and "the carefully and often delicately dressed *ixiptla*." The latter

What and Where Was Tamoanchan?

Brian Fagan, a former anthropology professor at the University of California–Santa Barbara, here discusses scholarly disagreement over what the Aztecs' mythical paradise of Tamoanchan was and where it might have been located.

[T]he Aztecs'] oral traditions contain constant, repetitive references to the decline of Teotihuacan when their gods departed. They also refer to a mysterious place of fullness and abundance, a location associated with mist, water, jaguars, and plenty, a place named Tamoanchan. No two experts seem to agree on what *Tamoanchan* means. [Bernardino de] Sahagun said that the word meant "we seek our home," but his Nahuatl rendering may be incorrect. . . . All sorts of places have been associated with Tamoanchan, among them a fabled region named Tlalocan, in the coastal lowlands to the east, where the sun rose. Historian Nigel Davies argues that possibly two Tamoanchans existed, the first a mythical place associated with the distant Gulf Coast, the second a more specific location, perhaps the general area where the city of Teotihuacan came into being. As time passed, Davies believes, Teotihuacan itself became the revered symbol of a magnificent civilization that had vanished forever, the cradle of the gods, Tamoanchan itself, the place where the Fifth Sun was born.

Brian Fagan. *The Aztecs*. New York: Freeman, 1984, pp. 36–37.

were people who dressed up like specific gods who it was thought sometimes dwelled in Tamoanchan. The splendor of these ceremonies, Wake goes on, also included "the exquisitely fashioned headdresses and richly embroidered mantles [cloaks] of the nobles," and exotic objects and animals, among them "precious plumes" of the brilliantly colored quetzal bird, "gems, rare seashells, jaguars, and alligators."[31] Such was the striking pageantry and spectacle in which the Aztecs regularly took part to honor the divine beings who, they believed, had created them from bones and blood.

CHAPTER 4

Great Journey: The Legend of Aztec Origins

T he national flag of modern Mexico displays a tense, exciting scene. Perched on a cactus plant that springs from a rock, a giant eagle thrashes violently, locked in a death struggle with a squirming serpent. That unique, distinctive image was not the handiwork of a contemporary artist, as many people assume. Instead, it comes directly from Aztec mythology. In fact, few cases of an ancient myth influencing the culture and lives of people in a later society are as clear-cut and dramatic as this one is. The legend from which the scene of the eagle on the cactus comes is one of the most crucial of all the Aztecs' myths, in large part because it explains their origins as a people.

The First Anthropologist

As was the case with other surviving Aztec myths, the written version of the one about the people's origins—often called the "Great Journey"—was compiled in the mid- to late 1500s, shortly after the Spaniards had conquered and dismantled the Aztec Empire. In the wake of that epic event, Bernardino de Sahagun, Diego Duran, and a few other fascinated Spanish priest-scholars stepped in. They made a concerted effort to preserve as much Aztec knowledge as possible. That included many of the myths, as well as aspects of religion, language, history, genealogy, astronomy, time-keeping methods, and other facets of traditional culture. For his part, Sahagun gathered the vast amounts of information he had collected into a volume that is today called the *Florentine Codex: General History of the Things of New Spain*. Later, in the twentieth century, his impressive studies of an entire native culture earned him the well-deserved nickname of "the first anthropologist" of the Americas.

A page from the Florentine Codex of Bernardino de Sahagun depicts Aztecs processing their fancy feathers. Sahagun's work was aimed at recording the Aztec culture for posterity.

In writing down the stories told in the myths, Sahagun and his fellow chroniclers were fortunate that they received the cooperation of many of the conquered natives. They interviewed a number of Aztec nobles and a few commoners as well, asking questions and recording answers in Nahuatl, rather than Spanish. As Michael E. Smith says, that astute and prudent approach "preserved much of the Aztec point of view."[32] In addition, Aztec society had a group of individuals who were specially trained in organizing and safeguarding the people's collected wisdom. Bernardino de Sahagun described these men, called *tlamatinime*, whom he greatly respected and admired, saying of each, "His are the black and red ink [that is, the writings]. His are the illustrated manuscripts. He studies the illustrated manuscripts. He himself is writing and wisdom. He is the path, the true way for others. He directs people and things. He is a guide in human affairs. [His] is the handed-down wisdom. He teaches it. He follows the path of truth."[33]

Based on what the nobles and *tlamatinime* said about the Aztecs' origins, more than twenty versions of the Great Journey were composed in the first century following the conquest alone. These included accounts by Duran and other Spaniards, as well as one by King Motecuhzoma II's own grandson, Don Fernando de Alvarado Tezozomoc. Although each telling of the myth differed from the others in some details, they all agreed on certain main points. All stated that the Mexica/Aztecs originally came from a land called Aztlan, lying far to the north of the Valley of Mexico. After many years of migration, adventure, and overcoming all sorts of obstacles and mishaps, they finally reached Lake Texcoco and not long afterward established their capital city of Tenochtitlan.

In examining these events, it is vital to point out the myth's unusually high degree of historicity, or historical authenticity. Although this story has come down through the ages in the form of a myth, many modern historians agree that several parts of it are closely based on real events. Linguistic, archaeological, and other evidence suggests that the Aztecs did migrate into central Mexico from somewhere to the north, for instance. As a result, most experts think that Aztlan may well have been a real place. They continue to search for its location as well as to discover whether other incidents described in the myth are garbled recollections of actual events.

Where Was Aztlan?

The Mexica/Aztecs, the tale of the Great Journey says, long ago dwelled in Aztlan, along with other groups of Nahuatl speakers, among them the Tlaxcalans, Tepanecas, and Acolhuas. Aztlan was composed in part of an island surrounded by water. (Modern scholars point out that when the Aztecs later built Tenochtitlan on an island in a lake, they may have been trying to re-create the setting of their ancestral home.) On the shore of the lake stood a mountain called Colhuacatepec, which meant "twisted hill." Inside that sacred mountain were seven caves collectively called Chicomoztoc. Together, the island, mountain, and caves made up Aztlan, the home of the Nahuatl-speaking peoples, including the Aztecs.

Modern historians are not the only ones who have tried to track down the location of Aztlan. According to Duran, King Motecuhzoma I, who ruled in the century before the Spaniards landed in Mexico, was intent on finding his people's initial homeland. That, he hoped, would prove the claims made in the myth. It would also establish a sacred spot for religious pilgrims to visit, as the sacred cities of Teotihuacan and Tollan already were. To these ends, Motecuhzoma sent several scholars and warriors on an expedition to locate Aztlan. They did find a lake with an island in it and a mountain rising on a nearby shore. But its exact location was somehow lost in the years just prior to the Spanish conquest.

Modern experts have suggested several possible geographical areas and sites for the historical Aztlan, if it did indeed exist. Most of these places are in north-central and east-central Mexico. One of the more intriguing and promising locations, however, is farther north, in the

A Sister People

According to Aztec myths, the Acolhuas, a people who joined in the triple alliance with the Aztecs in the 1400s, were a group of Nahuatl speakers who left Aztlan and journeyed into central Mexico before the Aztecs did.

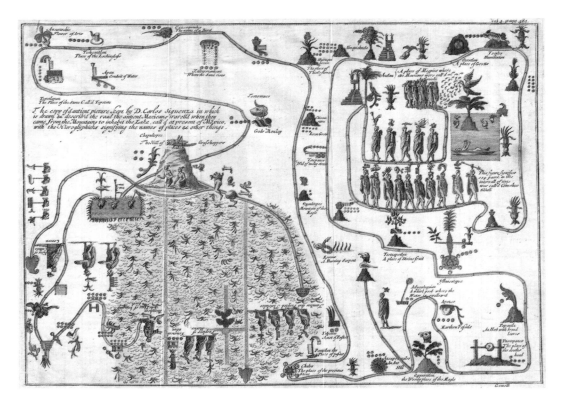

This early eighteenth-century map depicts the Aztecs supposed migration from mythical Aztlan to central Mexico.

southwestern United States. Some scholars point to a close connection between Nahuatl and the language spoken by the Utes, a Native American people who lived in Utah and Colorado. That appears to be evidence, they say, that the Aztecs originated in that same area and later migrated southward into Mexico.

Northern Arizona University archaeologist Kelley Hays-Gilpin goes a step further. She suggests that the folk who would later become the Aztecs first lived in central Mexico, perhaps as early as 3000 B.C. At some point, she proposes, they migrated northward into Arizona and Utah. Then, after living there for many centuries, they journeyed southward, back into Mexico, and it was that last migration that was remembered in the famous myth of Aztec origins.

The War God Speaks

Wherever the real Aztlan may have been, the legend of the Great Journey claims that the gods ordered some of the Nahuatl speakers to leave and find a new homeland to the south. The first of those peoples to move away, the Xochimilcas, supposedly did so in a year that corresponds to A.D. 820 in modern Western chronology. Each successive group of Nahuatl speakers departed, traveled southward into central Mexico, and there established its own city-state alongside those of existing local peoples. These early Mexican states, Brian Fagan writes, were "centered on small cities with impressive monumental architecture. Each [city-state] traded with its neighbors and maintained far-reaching exchange networks with areas outside the Valley [of Mexico]. The various states vied with each other, attempting to enlarge their domains through conquest and a complex network of political alliances."[34]

Meanwhile, back in Aztlan, the Mexica/Aztecs, finally received a communication from their fierce war god, Huitzilopochtli. He told them it was their turn to migrate southward and assured them that he would be at their side. They could establish towns from time to time along the way, he said, build houses in them, and settle down. They would be expected to raise crops and animals as needed to sustain themselves. But these settlements would be temporary, the god cautioned. In each case, after a few years—ten or fifteen at most—the people should move on, because their destiny was to establish a new and great city, and an empire as well. When the time was right, Huitzilopochtli declared, he would give them a sign that they had reached the spot where that city should rise. It would consist of a big eagle sitting atop a cactus growing out of a rock. There, he told them,

> we shall find our rest, our comfort, our grandeur. There our name will be praised and our Aztec nation made great. The might of our arms will be known and the courage of our brave hearts. . . . We shall become lords of gold and silver, of jewels and precious stones, [and we will] call this place Tenochtitlan. There we will build the city that is to be queen, that is to rule over all others in the country.[35]

The Aztec-Ute Connection

Northern Arizona University scholar Kelley Hays-Gilpin is among several modern experts who see a connection between the Aztecs' language and that of the Utes, an Indian tribe native to Utah and Colorado. This supports the idea that the Aztecs might have originated in the American West.

Was Huitzilopochtli Originally Mortal?

The origins of the Aztecs' patron god Huitzilopochtli, who later became a major Mesoamerican deity, are obscure, said the late Nigel Davies, one of the leading historians of pre-Spanish Mexico. Perhaps, he convincingly speculated, that character was originally a person—a leader and/ or a hero—and over the course of many centuries his legend grew until he entered Mexica/Aztec mythology as a god. Many precedents for this exist in world mythology, including the early Egyptian architect Imhotep, who one thousand years later was worshipped as a god. "If a certain deity predominates at the end of a long migration," Davies wrote in one of his twelve academic works,

the chronicles assume that the same god was paramount at the outset. Huitzilopochtli is described as in command [of the wandering Aztecs] right from the start. Yet his "birth" in Coetepec is described as if he had not existed before the Mexica arrived there. An element of contradiction is clearly present. It would therefore seem much more likely that the original leader called Huitzilopochtli was not a god but a mortal who had died. Mention is made in more than one source of a human leader of that name. One may thus suppose that a hero of early times became first a legend, then a deity. In fact, it was nothing new for a human leader to bear the name of a god.

Nigel Davies. *The Aztecs: A History.* Norman: University of Oklahoma Press, 1980, p. 17.

Huitzilopochtli accepts a blood sacrifice from Aztec worshippers. Historians have speculated that the god may have originally been a real person.

As the Great Journey began, on a date equivalent to about 1122, the people made sure to bring along a statue of Huitzilopochtli so that they would feel comforted by his presence. Duran reported that the idol was kept in a container made of river reeds. He added that the priests removed and displayed the statue whenever they felt it was necessary to remind the people that they must keep faith with the god and follow his rules. The fact that that deity traveled with and was so intimately linked with the early Aztecs shows that at this time he was still solely their personal patron deity. He was not yet a member of the central Mexican pantheon of gods and certainly not one of the leaders of that divine group, as he would eventually become.

Indeed, only later, when the Aztecs rose to prominence in the Valley of Mexico, did Huitzilopochtli gain major stature in Mesoamerican religion and mythology. This demonstrates that "the Aztecs had a dynamic, evolving religion," Michael E. Smith points out. In fact, he says, its "elements had yet to be fully synthesized [pieced together] and integrated when the Spaniards arrived in 1519."[36]

Temporary Towns

Following Huitzilopochtli's instructions, the Aztecs made their way southward, stopping now and then to create houses, farms, and small religious temples. The houses employed the same basic design and materials as those they would later build in Tenochtitlan. They were of two main types—those in which commoners lived and those where the far less numerous nobles dwelled.

The residences of ordinary folk were generally small, only rarely having more than a couple of rooms. The chief material used was clay bricks, made by packing the clay into wooden molds and leaving them out in the sun to dry. The main room featured a central hearth used primarily for warmth on cold nights, although some families also cooked on it. Others kept a similar hearth in a kitchen located in another room or in a separate tiny hut situated a few feet from the main one. Each hearth consisted of a fire made on top of a pile of rocks. Family members slept on woven reed mats and spread similar mats on the floor to function as carpets. The only furniture in the modern sense took the form of a few low chairs or stools constructed of reeds and some wooden chests in which people kept their clothes and other personal belongings.

Aztec nobles had larger, more spacious, two-story homes, usually built on stone bases. The walls were made of clay bricks, fieldstones, or a mix of the two, often covered by a layer of plaster. There were several rooms—including a dining area, bedchambers, and a meeting room, all surrounding a central courtyard open to the sky and the weather. The courtyards commonly featured sitting areas, bathing pools, and well-kept gardens.

Because they were relatively small and used easily available natural materials, these sorts of houses, even those of the well-to-do, did not take long to build. So when the Aztecs spent several years in one place, it was not difficult for them to erect a moderate-size town. Along with their nearby fields of crops and corrals for domesticated animals, such communities met all of their immediate needs.

One of these temporary towns, Patzcuaro, arose beside a lagoon, making it look somewhat like Aztlan. So some of the Aztecs became confused and thought they may have reached their final destination. Speaking for the god, however, the priests claimed this was not the right spot, and after a few years, on the insistence of Huitzilopochtli, the people resumed their migration.

Divine Wrath

Later, at a mountain called Catepec, the Aztecs diverted a river's waters, creating an artificial lake. They built a settlement there, which like earlier versions had clusters of brick houses and small farms. What made this time different was that, after a few years in that unusually pleasant spot, some of the people, including several priests, rebelled against the long-standing plan and decided to stay permanently. They also went so far as to stop worshipping Huitzilopochtli, which made him extremely angry. According to the story, as told by Duran and several other sixteenth-century chroni-

clers, one day the god appeared in the town and in his wrath punished the rebels by ripping out their hearts.

Many modern historians think this part of the myth was a mangled memory of a real event in which two rival groups of the migrating Aztecs fought for supremacy. The group that won apparently believed that the defeated rebels had betrayed the patron god, as well as the people as a whole. It was therefore seen as justified that they be punished in an unusually harsh manner—having their hearts torn out. This extreme measure would certainly have been carried out under the rationale that it was the god's will. As such, it was a religious ceremony, which required solemn, formal rituals, and accordingly, numerous scholars see this as the beginning of the Aztecs' infamous custom of human sacrifice.

After leaving Mount Catepec, the Mexica/Aztecs continued their southward voyage until, sometime in the late 1200s, they reached the northern edge of the enormous Lake Texcoco. They saw that the area was inhabited by several well-established peoples, all of which were stronger than

Aztec nobles lived in houses such as this one reconstructed by modern scientists.

A New Tribe Is Born

The myth of the Great Journey is composed of numerous sub-myths, one of which tells how, during their centuries-long trek, the Mexica/Aztecs allowed some of their number to separate from the main group and become autonomous, or independent. This version is told by noted Mexican American scholar Manuel Aguilar-Moreno.

The beauty of the lagoon at Patzcuaro allured even the most loyal high priests and they conducted elaborate rituals to consult Huitzilopochtli and ask if he would allow them to remain in Patzcuraro. The divine response was unenthusiastic. However, the high priests asked permission to allow a small group of people to remain in Patzcuaro. To this petition, Huitzilopochtli responded very benevolently and told his high priests that they should remain alert, and when a group of people of various ages entered the lagoon to bathe, they should hide their clothes and immediately abandon the town. The Mexica did so. They abandoned Patzcuaro while some members of their tribe bathed. When the unsuspecting villagers emerged from the lagoon, they found themselves naked and abandoned. Not knowing where to go, they stayed, [and] later became an autonomous tribe known as the Tarascans, direct descendants of the Mexica.

Manuel Aguilar-Moreno. *Handbook to Life in the Aztec World.* New York: Oxford University Press, 2006, p. 33.

they were. So they kept on moving, slowly skirting the lake's western shore. In time they came to a place called Chapultepec (meaning "Grasshopper Hill") and erected a walled village in order to protect themselves from the many natives who clearly did not want them there.

The locals were so hostile, in fact, that the wall was not enough to stop their periodic assaults. The Aztecs were therefore forced once again to move on. They rounded the lake's southern rim, and on its eastern shore they came to the city of Colhuacan. Its ruler looked at the bedraggled travelers and, unlike so many others in the region, took pity on them. He allowed the Aztecs to camp on a small, barren, snake-infested piece of his land, and there they worked hard to make it as habitable and hospitable as they could. As in the past, they erected simple houses and grew the crops they needed to survive. A few years later, however, they had a serious disagreement with the ruler who had befriended them, and as a result they had to abandon their newest homes still again.

Special in the Gods' Eyes

The weary Aztecs' seemingly endless trek continued until a date corresponding to the year 1325. While roaming along the lakeshore, trying to steer clear of unfriendly local towns, they came upon an area with unusually clear water and much lush and beautiful vegetation. Huitzilopochtli told them that at last they had reached the place that would be their home forever. Soon after the god had spoken to them, the story goes, the people looked toward the shore and saw something that took their breath away. It was a large rock with a prickly pear cactus growing from its top. Above the cactus "stood the eagle," as Duran told it, "with its wings stretched out toward the rays of the sun, basking in their warmth and the freshness of the morning." When the Aztecs saw what was clearly Huitzilopochtli's prophecy and promise coming true,

> they humbled themselves, making reverences [bowing down] as if the bird were a divine thing. The eagle, seeing them, also humbled himself, bowing his head low in their direction. As the Aztecs observed the actions of the eagle, they realized they had come to the end of their journey, so they began to weep and dance about with joy and contentment. In thanksgiving, they said, "By what right do we deserve such good fortune? Who made us worthy of such grace, such excellence, and greatness?"[37]

The jubilant Aztecs proceeded to answer their own question. It was their divine patron and protector who had made them worthy and brought them to this place of their destiny. Clearly, they concluded, to be deliberately singled out and aided that way by a mighty god, they must be a special people. This aspect of the myth strikingly reflects still another reality of Aztec society and life. Having the prophecy come true after the passage of several generations of hard work and hardships made the Aztecs in the story feel not only successful, but also exceptional as a people. They came to believe that they and their nation were superior to all other peoples and lands.

Taking these events in the myth quite seriously, the real Aztecs developed similar feelings of exceptionalism, seeing themselves as somehow special in the eyes of the gods. This greatly contributed to their spectacular successes in the two centuries following the establishment of their city on an island in Lake Texcoco. Their city-state was small at first, and for a while neighboring states remained militarily stronger. Moreover, those neighbors owned the land on which that new city-state rested, so the Aztecs had to pay heavy taxes as a form of rent for using the land.

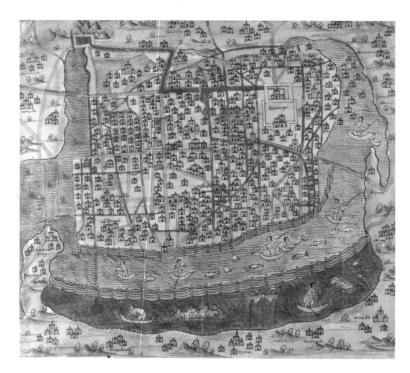

This 1560 map shows Tenochtitlan surrounded by Lake Texcoco. The god Huitzilopochtli told the Aztecs to live here.

Over time, however, Huitzilopochtli's chosen people grew in number and developed a strong army of their own. In 1428 they joined forces with two other local peoples and defeated the powerful state that had recently been levying crippling taxes on Tenochtitlan. That triple alliance long remained in effect. But by 1500 the Aztecs had come to overshadow the other two members and had built a large empire that stretched far to the east and west.

Moreover, Tenochtitlan was no small collection of brick and stone huts, as earlier Mexica/Aztec towns had been. In addition to thousands of individual homes, both big and small, the new capital had huge stone-floored plazas lined with towering stone pyramids, each topped by one or two magnificent temples. The Great Journey described in the myth had in many ways merged with the Aztecs' real-life, centuries-long migration from far to the north. These determined, industrious people had managed to transform themselves from a little-known, much-despised tribe into the widely feared rulers of an expansive, powerful kingdom. It appeared they were invincible. But then, out of nowhere, bearded strangers from far across the sea arrived, and even the great Huitzilopochtli was no match for the guns, diseases, and deception they brought.

CHAPTER 5

Plumed Serpent: Aztec Myths in Pop Culture

The sprawling Aztec Empire had existed for barely a century when in 1519 the Spanish expedition led by Hernán Cortés arrived on Mexico's eastern coast. One of the leading conquistadors, or Spanish soldier-adventurers, of that era, he did not see the Aztec civilization as a potential ally, trade partner, and source of new knowledge. Much of world history since that time would have been very different if he had.

Instead, Cortés and other Spaniards and Europeans looked on the Aztecs and their native neighbors as heathens and inferiors to be exploited. Although the newcomers from across the sea came with smiles on their faces and promises of friendship, from the start they had a simple, straightforward plan to invade and conquer. First they would strip the Mesoamerican natives of their gold, gems, and other valuables. Then they would take possession of or destroy their cities. Finally, they would send out missionaries who would teach the natives that their religious beliefs, including their cherished myths, were childish and wrongheaded and that Christianity was the only true faith.

Yet, although the intruders did inflict untold damage and misery and bring about the downfall of the Aztecs' nation and empire, they did not kill the natives' spirit. Nor did the

Spaniards manage to eradicate all of the Aztecs' religious beliefs and myths. Many native books and other sources of traditional knowledge and culture were burned, to be sure. But the handful of humanitarian Spanish priests headed by Bernardino de Sahagun and Diego Duran contradicted that policy and chose to preserve, rather than destroy, Aztec culture. Also, numerous literate natives kept various aspects of their traditional civilization, among them the major myths, alive. So to some degree that ancient and venerable culture survived. It remained a potent undercurrent in Mexican society and life in the years that followed; and in the twentieth century, images and concepts from Aztec religion and mythology exploded into popular culture, scorching themselves into the creative arts and public consciousness.

Hernán Cortés, like most Europeans, looked upon the Aztecs and other natives as heathens and inferiors to be subjugated and exploited.

Calculated Lies

This fateful, centuries-long transformation of traditional Aztec culture began when Motecuhzoma first received reports about the appearance of peculiar strangers on Mexico's eastern shores. (Over time, that ruler's name was cor-

An eighteenth-century manuscript illustration depicts the Aztec king Motecuhzoma.

rupted into *Montezuma*, a spelling often seen today.) One messenger told the king that some odd-looking men had climbed out of "two towers or small mountains floating on the waves of the sea." After fishing for a while from a small boat, the messenger said, the foreigners had climbed back into the towers. "There were about fifteen of these people," he told Motecuhzoma, "some with blue jackets, others with red." They "have very light skin, much lighter than ours. They all have long beards, and their hair comes only to their ears."[38]

What the Aztec ruler did not yet know was that these strangers were men from a distant country called Spain. They were led by Cortés, then thirty-five, who in 1506 had migrated to the Spanish colony on the island of Hispaniola, in what is now the Caribbean Sea. Later he had moved to the Spanish colony in Cuba and become wealthy from cattle ranching. That had made him socially prominent enough to acquire the command of an impending expedition to the Mexican coast, which at the time was little known and even mysterious. In February 1519 Cortés left Cuba with eleven vessels. They held some 530 European soldiers and other personnel and a few hundred Cuban natives, along with 20 cannons and 16 horses.

At first Motecuhzoma decided not to attack the outsiders, who steadily made their way to the southern shore of Lake Texcoco. Cortés guided his followers along one of the impressive stone causeways that led to Tenochtitlan and approached one of the city's gates. They could see that thousands of natives had climbed onto rooftops and were silently staring down at them. After a while, some Aztec officials came out and greeted the strangers; then Motecuhzoma himself appeared, and he and Cortés exchanged gifts. Through an interpreter, the Spaniard told the great king, "We are [your] friends. There is nothing to fear. We have wanted to see [you] for a long time, and now we have seen [your] face and heard [your] words. [We] love [you] well and our hearts are contented."[39]

As history would soon show, nearly everything Cortés said was a lie calculated to keep the Aztecs in the dark about his real plans. In the months that followed, he repaid Motecuhzoma's trust by taking him hostage and forcing him to reveal where all of his gold and other valuables were stored.

Shortly afterward, a group of Cortés's soldiers ambushed and slaughtered hundreds of Aztecs while they were engaged in a solemn religious ceremony. Then Cortés had Motecuhzoma and the rest of the Aztec nobles strangled to death. In a sense adding insult to injury, one of the Spaniards unknowingly passed on smallpox germs to the natives, who died by the thousands. Even the new Aztec king, Cuitlahuac, perished from that terrifying and lethal illness.

A Powerful Merger of Old and New

Eventually, the invaders captured Tenochtitlan, and soon the Aztec nation ceased to exist, at least in the official sense. The Spaniards rapidly turned central Mexico into their newest colony, Nueva España, or New Spain, with Cortés in the governor's seat. In addition, much of the once mighty metropolis of Tenochtitlan was leveled to make way for the new Spanish capital of Mexico City.

Nevertheless, traditional Aztec culture, including many of its myths, survived this horrific holocaust. Many of the natives doggedly clung to their old beliefs and ways in hopes of preserving their identity as a people. First they continued to speak Nahuatl and to pen accounts of their lifestyle and ongoing history in that language.

They also held on to some aspects of their traditional religion, including many of their old myths. True, over time most of the mestizos—natives who intermarried with criollos, Spaniards who were born in New Spain—converted to Christianity, more specifically Catholicism. But the conversion process was almost never complete. This was because the Aztecs' native faith was, as Manuel Aguilar-Moreno puts it, "a complex, deeply rooted agricultural religion profoundly ingrained in the fabric of native life."[40] So it was nearly impossible to erase all aspects of that ancient faith from the intellectual roots of the indigenous peoples. That was especially true with engaging stories like those in the myths, which passed down through the generations by word of mouth—usually from parents to children in the privacy of home life. "Superficially, the Indians were attracted to the elaborate rituals and colorful ceremonies of the Catholic church," Brian Fagan explains.

But a simple transfer of allegiance [from the old gods to the new one] was simply impossible. The friars were unable to get across the deeper meaning of Christian doctrine, the significance of such abstract concepts as virtue and sin. Many Indians simply added God to their pantheon of deities and counted the saints as members of an anthropomorphic [human-like] pantheon of lesser gods. The hardest belief [for the natives] to shake was the notion that the gods had to be sustained by humans with [sacrificial offerings].[41]

The result was that over the centuries, Catholicism in Mexico came to be a blending, or syncretism, of old and new religious beliefs and rituals. The widely popular modern Mexican holiday called the Day of the Dead, for instance, is a combination of elements from the Catholic All Souls' Day and the Aztec autumn festival, which paid homage to

Some Striking Religious Similarities

The traditional Aztec religion and Christianity, which most Aztecs adopted in the century or so following the Spanish conquest, had a number of differences. The most obvious was that the native faith had multiple gods and Christianity only one. Yet the similarities between the two religions are striking and surprising to many people today. Both revolve around a divine act of sacrifice, for example. In Christianity, Jesus suffers a horrible death by crucifixion in order to save humanity, whereas in the Aztec religion the gods suffer an equally terrible death by burning, also to save humanity. Moreover, both faiths have stories about a great flood that wreaked havoc on humanity. The Christian ver-

sion features God warning an old man named Noah, who builds an enormous boat in which he and his wife ride out the deluge. In the Aztec version, Chalchiuhtlicue, goddess of lakes, rivers, and oceans, warns a man named Coxcox and his wife, Xochiquetzal. They construct a big canoe from a hollowed-out log, which allows them to survive. Still another close parallel between the two belief systems consists of tales about wars in heaven. In the Christian version, God and his "good" angels fight and defeat Satan and the "bad" angels. The Aztecs had myths about four wars in which the gods Quetzalcoatl and Tezcatlipoca opposed each other—one conflict for each of the first four worlds, or Suns.

deceased ancestors. In preparation for celebrating the Day of the Dead, people erect colorful outdoor altars in which Aztec mythology often plays a part. It is common, for example, to include artistic renderings of the canine character Xolotl, from the myth of Quetzalcoatl's creation of humanity. "If you look closely at these altars," David Carrasco writes, "you may notice a humorous, tender image of the Aztec spirit-dog Xolotl, standing on a pedestal by the underground river on the way to Mictlan, waiting to guide the souls of the dead to the other shore. These celebratory altars emphasize the Aztec image of death and regeneration rather than the contrary image of sacrifice and conquest."[42]

Similarly, both the mestizos and full-blooded natives, called Nahuas, came to associate the Christian Virgin Mary with the Aztec mother goddess Coatlicue. In one of the old myths, she gave birth to the moon and stars. A powerful merger of those two sacred female figures was the Virgin of Guadalupe, who is still worshipped extensively in Mexico.

Rivera and the Muralists

Other aspects of Aztec religion and mythology have also inspired modern popular culture (sometimes called "pop culture"), including the work of painters, sculptors, composers, and novelists and other writers. Painters, especially muralists, have been particularly prominent. After a great deal of political and social upheaval during the so-called Mexican Revolution, lasting roughly from 1910 to 1920, the Mexican government looked for ways to promote patriotism and acceptance of modern social ideals. One of these was the notion that the mestizos, most of whom were poor and landless, were as worthy of land ownership and political power as the traditional wealthy Spanish landowners were. One way to celebrate the common people was to cover the walls of government buildings with giant paintings showing modern Mexicans' connection to their past—including their Aztec roots.

The Virgin on the Hilltop

The widespread worship of the Virgin of Guadalupe was largely based on an Aztec man's 1531 claim that he encountered that caring goddess wearing shining robes on a sacred hilltop.

The most famous figure in this muralist movement was artist Diego Rivera (1886–1957), who outside of his work became controversial for his drinking, partying, and womanizing. Widely viewed as one of the leading painters of the twentieth century, he completed numerous huge wall paintings in both Mexico and the United States. One, which graces Mexico City's National Palace, consists of a stunning panorama of the Aztec capital of Tenochtitlan at the height of its power and glory, shortly before the arrival of the Spaniards.

Rivera's works are noted for showing all sorts of characters from different time periods—some historical, others mythical—crowded together as if they were contemporary

Famed Mexican painter Diego Rivera's mural of Tenochtitlan is in the National Palace in Mexico City.

comrades. For example, some of his murals depict Quetzalcoatl and other ancient gods standing beside real-life political leaders. Other Rivera paintings employ mythical symbols and magical beliefs to make political points. One of the more interesting examples is the *Indian Warrior*, completed in 1931. In the words of one expert observer:

> The viewer's eyes are met by those of an Aztec warrior clad in a jaguar mask and skin, triumphantly stabbing an armored *conquistador* in the throat. For the ancient Aztecs, the jaguar symbolized power, and they believed wearing its mask or skin could impart superhuman abilities. Though the outcome of the Spanish conquest is well known, in showing the Aztec warrior as triumphant, Rivera here inverted [reversed] the historical power relationship to elevate Mexico's pre-[conquest] roots.[43]

The Royal Shakespeare Company and the National Theater of Mexico perform Luis Mario Moncada's play A Soldier in Every Son *in Mexico City, a play about the pre-conquest Aztec Empire.*

Novels, Plays, Movies, and Games

Following the example of painters, writers have also incorporated Aztec myths into their own popular works. The most

famous example was the great English author D.H. Lawrence (1885–1930). While living in New Mexico during the 1920s, he paid some extended visits to Mexico, and the colorful mix of ethnic groups there fascinated him.

In particular, Lawrence was captivated by the power of religion and myths in ancient Aztec society, and he explored that theme in his now renowned novel *The Plumed Serpent*. Published in 1925, its original title was *Quetzalcoatl*, a mythical character mentioned often in the book. The story concerns a group of modern intellectuals who try to revive the ancient Aztec religion, including its pantheon of gods, in hopes of gaining political power.

That same theme—a political leader using people's belief in gods and myths to sustain his power—has also been explored onstage. In 2012 England's famed Royal Shakespeare Company teamed up with the National Theater of Mexico. As part of the World Shakespeare Festival, they staged Mexican playwright Luis Mario Moncada's *A Soldier in Every Son*. This massive production focuses on a thirty-year period in preconquest Mexico in which the Aztecs used military might, marriage alliances, and the exploitation of religion and mythology to forge an empire.

Another vibrant, imaginative written work inspired by Aztec mythology is *Servant of the Underworld*, a novel by Aliette de Bodard released in 2010. Like Moncada's play, Bodard's story takes place in Mexico before the Spanish conquest. The main character is an Aztec high priest named Acatl, who conducts the regular sacrifices to the dark deity of the underworld, Mictlantecuhtli. Acatl is informed of a death in the community that may be related to magic spells. Reluctantly, he investigates, which leads him to some disturbing discoveries involving mystical powers and human intrigue.

Two other modern novels involve the Aztec mother goddess, Coatlicue, whose postconquest popularity was based on her connection to the Virgin Mary. In Harry Harrison's *Captive Universe* (1969), set in humanity's future, an Aztec-like culture develops inside a vast spaceship. Some areas of that craft are protected by a robot that displays Coatlicue's unique traits and personality. Another novel with an off-beat premise, Neil Gaiman's *American Gods* (2001), finds the spirit of the same goddess inhabiting her statue in a modern museum.

Coatlicue has also appeared frequently in other works of pop culture. One is the 1978 horror movie *Mardi Gras Massacre*, in which a man claiming to be an Aztec priest sacrifices young women to the goddess. Two others are Camelot Software and Nintendo's 2002 role-playing video game *Golden Sun: The Lost Age* and its 2010 sequel, *Golden Sun: Dark Dawn*.

From Superhero to Flying Dragon

Several other characters from Aztec mythology appear in modern books, movies, and games. But none have been incorporated into popular culture as often as the colorful Feathered Serpent, Quetzalcoatl. Lawrence's use of him in *The Plumed Serpent* was only one of several appearances of that god in novels, an outstanding example of which is the 2010 science fiction book *City of the Gods: The Return of Quetzalcoatl*. In novelist Patrick Garone's complex plot, Quetzalcoatl starts out as the human ruler of the giant Mesoamerican city of Teotihuacan but later transforms into a fierce dragon-like beast. He reawakens in modern times to aid humanity in its fight against invading aliens.

Leaping from traditional novel to graphic novel, in 1996 Quetzalcoatl became a recurring character in the DC Comics series *Aztek*. The title refers to a superhero who acts as Quetzalcoatl's champion on earth, usually in battles against that god's archenemy in Aztec mythology, the dark and destructive deity Tezcatlipoca. Here, DC made an attempt to employ some of the themes and ideas in the original myths, while exploiting the characters within the context of that company's established universe of heroes and villains.

Quetzalcoatl has been particularly popular in film, with numerous television shows and movies to his credit. Many in the enormous legion of *Star Trek* fans still remember his appearance

The Smoking Mirror on Windows

Quetzalcoatl's divine nemesis, Tezcatlipoca, is the lead character in the video game *Broken Sword II: Smoking Mirror*, which appeared on Microsoft Windows OS X in 2010 and on Android in 2012.

An Aztec God in New York

The character of the major Aztec god Quetzalcoatl has been exploited in numerous modern novels, paintings, television shows, movies, and video games. Several of these have portrayed him in large degree just as the Aztecs viewed him—as a flying serpent or dragon-like being. One of the more memorable examples was the 1982 feature film *Q* (at times released as *Q—the Winged Serpent*), written and directed by Larry Cohen. Set in the modern era, the story deals with a secret Aztec religious cult that is connected to a series of grisly murders in New York City. Two detectives investigate and discover that the crimes were committed by a monstrous winged lizard that dwells inside the metal spire atop the famous Chrysler Building. A second-rate crook, played by Michael Moriarty, also find the creature's lair. Eventually, the police lead a military assault on and kill Quetzalcoatl, but they fail to find an egg it has recently hatched, which leaves the story open to a sequel. (No such follow-up has so far been made).

Director Larry Cohen's 1982 movie Q, the Winged Serpent *has a flying lizard terrorizing New York City.*

in "How Sharper than a Serpent's Tooth," an episode from the 1973 animated *Trek* series. Similarly, the many fans of the *Stargate* franchise recall "Crystal Skull" (2000), an episode from the third season of *Stargate SG-1*, in which Quetzalcoatl takes the form of a huge alien being. Still another memorable TV turn for the ancient Aztec divinity was "Bird of Paradise," an episode of the short-lived 1998 show *Godzilla: The Series*. This time the old god was a fire-breathing

Acclaimed English novelist and poet D.H. Lawrence wrote a novel about Quetzalcoatl titled The Plumed Serpent.

dinosaur-like creature that springs to life inside an ancient volcano.

Quetzalcoatl's frequent appearances within the realm of pop culture as a dragon or other giant reptilian monster has actually proved justified. In 1971 Douglas A. Lawson, then a graduate student at the University of Texas, discovered the remains of a prehistoric pterosaur (a large flying reptile that coexisted with dinosaurs). Based on the mythical god's image as a feathered serpent, he named the creature *Quetzalcoatlus*, thereby introducing an element of Aztec mythology into modern science. (Although pterosaurs did not have feathers like those of modern birds, their skin was covered with small fibers that together looked like a coat of hair.)

Evidence suggests that some specimens of *Quetzalcoatlus* had wingspans of 33 feet (10m) or more.

In the Hearts of the People

Clearly, a major reason the divine characters of Aztec mythology have so often been adopted by the varied producers of mass-market pop culture is that these beings were larger than life. First, they displayed human-like emotions, including love, joy, anger, hate, jealousy, and desire. That made them understandable and appealing to the people who worshipped them. The gods also wielded great power, including the ability to manipulate nature's forces for either good or evil, and for that reason people frequently feared them. Furthermore, and very importantly, the Aztec deities did not merely manipulate and demand obedience and worship from humans. They

The flying dinosaur Quetzacoatalus was named for the Aztecs' feathered-serpent god.

also saw it as their duty to make the world habitable for their mortal creations, and they were willing to sacrifice their own lives to make that happen.

This high-minded trait of selflessness gives these divinities a moral compass, depth of personality, and truly heroic quality that lifts them above the two-dimensional level of the deities in a number of the world's other mythologies. It also explains why, following the Spanish conquest, many Aztecs could not bring themselves to completely abandon their traditional gods. When the Spaniards demanded that they simply replace those "false" deities with the Christian God, one group of Aztec priests responded, "There is life because of the gods. With their sacrifice, they gave us life." Yet now, based on Spanish insistence, "are we to destroy the ancient order of life?" With tears welling up in their eyes, the priests pleaded, "We know on whom life is dependent, on whom the perpetuation of the race depends," so please "do nothing to our people" that "will cause them to perish!"[44]

This extreme devotion to the life-giving beings of their ancient myths was the principal reason that many postconquest Aztecs held on to some of the old beliefs and often blended them with the Christian ones they ended up accepting. Thus, some of the Aztec gods and myths survived and remain alive today because many Mexicans simply refused to let them go. Carleton Beals summed up this emotionally moving reality, saying that though many of the old gods "receded into the mists of the past," several others "have been hidden behind the Christian altars. Many have lingered on in the remote countryside and in the hearts of the people. To this day, some have not died. And the fiery pottery and the legends that endangered them, that put prophecy on the lips of the common Mexican, still live on in the lives and hearts of many of the people."[45]

Introduction: Altering the Past to Explain the Present

1. Edith Hamilton. *Mythology.* New York: Grand Central, 1999, p. 13.
2. C.A. Burland and Werner Forman. *Feathered Serpent and Smoking Mirror: The Gods and Cultures of Ancient Mexico.* New York: Putnam, 1975, p. 58.
3. Quoted in Burland and Forman. *Feathered Serpent and Smoking Mirror,* p. 7.
4. Michael E. Smith. *The Aztecs.* Oxford, England: Blackwell, 2002, p. 283.
5. Susan D. Gillespie. *The Aztec Kings: The Constitution of Rulership in Mexica History.* Tucson: University of Arizona Press, 1992, pp. xxiii, xxviii.

Chapter 1: Enchanted Vision: The Aztecs and Their Gods

6. Bernal Diaz del Castillo. *The Conquest of New Spain.* Translated by J.M. Cohen. New York: Penguin, 1963, p. 214.
7. Smith. *The Aztecs,* p. 37.
8. Lewis Spence. "Mexican Mythology: Tezcatlipoca and the Toltecs." Internet Sacred Text Archive. www.sacred-texts.com/nam/mmp/mmp05.htm.
9. Guilhem Olivier. "The Gods of the Mexica (2)." Mexicolore. www.mexicolore.co.uk/aztecs/gods/gods-of-the-mexica-2.
10. Smith. *The Aztecs,* p. 211.
11. David Carrasco. *Daily Life of the Aztecs.* Santa Barbara, CA: ABC CLIO, 2011, p. 48.
12. Lora L. Kile. "Returning God or Blood Sacrifice: What Were Moctezuma's Intentions Toward Cortes?" Master's thesis, University of Missouri–Columbia, 2011, p. 51. https://mospace.umsystem.edu/xmlui/bitstream/handle/10355/11179/research.pdf?sequence=3.

Chapter 2: Life Out of Death: The Creation of the World

13. Norman Bancroft Hunt. *Gods and Myths of the Aztecs.* New York: Smithmark, 1996, p. 95.
14. Quoted in Miguel Leon-Portilla. *Aztec Thought and Culture: A Study of the Ancient Nahuatl Mind.* Norman: University of Oklahoma Press, 1990, p. 90.
15. Leon-Portilla, *Aztec Thought and Culture,* p. 31.
16. Leon-Portilla, *Aztec Thought and Culture,* p. 36.
17. Bernardino de Sahagun. *Florentine Codex: General History of the Things of New Spain.* Vol. 7. Translated by Arthur O. Anderson and Charles E. Dibble. Salt Lake City:

University of Utah Press, 1950–1969, p. 4.

18. Sahagun. *Florentine Codex*. Vol. 7, p. 6.

19. Smith. *The Aztecs*, p. 208.

20. Bernal Diaz del Castillo. *The Discovery and Conquest of Mexico, 1517–1521*. Translated by A.P. Maudslay. New York: Farrar, Straus, and Giroux, 1956, p. 436.

21. Carleton Beals. *Stories Told by the Aztecs Before the Spaniards Came*. London: Abelard Schuman, 1970, p. 37.

22. Philip Coppens. "Cuicuilco: The Oldest Pyramid on Earth?" *The New Pyramid Age*. www.philipcoppens.com/nap_art5.html.

Chapter 3: Descent into Hell: The Making of Humanity

23. Manuel Aguilar-Moreno. *Handbook to Life in the Aztec World*. New York: Oxford University Press, 2007, p. 165.

24. Aguilar-Moreno. *Handbook to Life in the Aztec World*, p. 165.

25. Quoted in Leon-Portilla. *Aztec Thought and Culture*, pp. 107–108.

26. Angel Vigil. *The Eagle and the Cactus: Traditional Stories from Mexico*. Englewood, CO: Libraries Limited, 2000, p. 53.

27. Brian Fagan. *The Aztecs*. New York: Freeman, 1984, p. 250.

28. Eleanor Wake. *Framing the Sacred: The Indian Churches of Early Colonial Mexico*. Norman: University of Oklahoma Press, 2010, p. 44.

29. Sahagun. *Florentine Codex*. Vol. 2, p. 202.

30. Sahagun. *Florentine Codex*. Vol. 3, p. 223.

31. Wake. *Framing the Sacred*, p. 44.

Chapter 4: Great Journey: The Legend of Aztec Origins

32. Smith. *The Aztecs*, p. 20.

33. Quoted in Leon-Portilla. *Aztec Thought and Culture*, p. 10.

34. Fagan. *The Aztecs*, p. 56.

35. Quoted in Diego Duran. *The History of the Indies of New Spain*. Translated by Doris Heyden. Norman: University of Oklahoma Press, 1994, pp. 43–44.

36. Smith. *The Aztecs*, p. 210.

37. Duran. *The History of the Indies of New Spain*, p. 44.

Chapter 5: Plumed Serpent: Aztec Myths in Pop Culture

38. Quoted in Miguel Leon-Portilla, ed. *The Broken Spears: The Aztec Account of the Conquest of Mexico*. Boston: Beacon, 1992, pp. 16–17.

39. Quoted in Leon-Portilla. *The Broken Spears*, pp. 64–65.

40. Aguilar-Moreno. *Handbook to Life in the Aztec World*, p. 388.

41. Fagan. *The Aztecs*, p. 295.

42. David Carrasco. *The Aztecs: A Very Short Introduction*. New York: Oxford University Press, 2012, p. 120.

43. Nina Agrawal. "Diego Rivera's Murals: Public Art Then and Now." *Americas Quarterly*, January 18, 2012. www.americasquarterly.org/node/3225.

44. Quoted in Leon-Portilla. *Aztec Thought and Culture*, pp. 64–66.

45. Beals. *Stories Told by the Aztecs Before the Spaniards Came*, p. 197.

Aztlan: The legendary homeland of the Aztecs before they began their journey into central Mexico.

calmecac: A school attended by the children of nobles.

chinampas: Fertile, raised gardens created in swampy terrain.

codex (plural is *codices*): A book.

conquistador: In late medieval times, one of a group of aggressive Spanish soldiers and adventurers.

cosmos: The universe, or all that exists.

criollos: In early New Spain, people born in Mexico but having Spanish parents and ancestry.

ixiptla: People who dressed up like specific gods, usually during religious ceremonies.

macehualtin: Commoners in Aztec society.

Mesoamerica: A modern term describing ancient central Mexico and neighboring regions.

mestizos: In early New Spain, people born of mixed marriages between natives and Spaniards.

Mexica: The original name of the Nahuatl-speaking group that people across the world later came to call the Aztecs.

Mictlan: In Aztec myths, the underworld.

Nahuatl: The language spoken by the Aztecs and some related Mesoamerican peoples.

sacrifice: An offering made to satisfy a god or gods.

syncretism: The blending or merger of ideas from two or more different religions.

Tenochtitlan: The Aztecs' capital, situated on an island in Lake Texcoco.

Teotihuacan: Located east of Lake Texcoco, the largely abandoned Mesoamerican city that the Aztecs believed was a home of the gods.

teteo **(singular is *teotl*):** The gods.

tlacotin: Aztec slaves.

tlamatinime: People specifically trained to organize and safeguard the Aztecs' collected knowledge, including their myths.

tlatoani: The Aztec king's title.

Valley of Mexico: A large, mountain-ringed basin in central Mexico.

xoloitzcuintle **(or *xolo*):** The scientific name for the Mexican hairless dog.

Books

Manuel Aguilar-Moreno. *Handbook to Life in the Aztec World.* New York: Oxford University Press, 2006. A fact-filled look at Aztec culture and everyday life.

David Carrasco. *Daily Life of the Aztecs.* Santa Barbara, CA: ABC CLIO, 2011. A thoughtful, easy-to-read account of life in the Aztec world by a leading scholar.

David Carrasco. *Quetzalcoatl and the Irony of Empire: Myth and Prophecies in the Aztec Tradition.* Boulder: University Press of Colorado, 2001. Although it is now more than a decade old, this book by a major Harvard University historian contains much interesting and still relevant analysis of surviving Aztec myths.

Anita Ganeri. *Mesoamerican Myth: A Treasury of Central American Legends, Art, and History.* Armonk, NY: Sharpe Focus, 2008. Aimed at junior high school readers, this is a beautifully illustrated, basic introduction to the subject.

Natalie Hyde. *Understanding Mesoamerican Myths.* New York: Crabtree, 2013. An easy-to-read summary of the main Aztec myths that will appeal to junior high and high school readers.

Miguel Leon-Portilla, ed. *The Broken Spears: The Aztec Account of the Conquest of Mexico.* Boston: Beacon, 2011. An excellent translation of several riveting surviving native accounts of the Spanish conquest of the Aztecs.

Charles Phillips and David M. Jones. *The Lost History of the Aztec and Maya.* London: Southwater, 2014. This splendidly illustrated book contains a large amount of factual information about Aztec culture, including its religion and myths.

Michael E. Smith. *The Aztecs.* Oxford, England: Blackwell, 2002. A major academic reviewer aptly called this volume "an enjoyable learning tool" and said it "will for long remain the best [available] introduction to the Aztecs' state and empire and to the society they constructed."

Richard F. Townsend. *The Aztecs.* London: Thames and Hudson, 2000. A superior, highly acclaimed study of this pivotal ancient people by a leading scholar.

Wilson G. Turner. *Aztec Designs.* Mineola, NY: Dover, 2009. Mythical Aztec characters abound in this rich collection of line drawings that can be reproduced and used as artistic templates for art projects, embroidery, beadwork, gifts, and so forth.

Angel Vigil. *The Eagle and the Cactus: Traditional Stories from Mexico*. Englewood, CO: Libraries Limited, 2000. Several classic Aztec myths are nicely retold here by Vigil, an award-winning Colorado educator and storyteller.

Websites

Aztec History (www.aztec-history.com). This handsome-looking site provides a wealth of information on the Aztecs, including a detailed but easy-to-read overview of the different "suns" involved in the Aztecs' complex creation myths.

Aztec Origins, About.com (http://archaeology.about.com/od/aztec archaeology/a/aztec_origins.htm). About.com: Archaeology provides this brief but useful synopsis of the Aztecs' myth-shrouded arrival in the Valley of Mexico; includes many links for more information.

Aztecs, Mexicolore (www.mexicolore .co.uk/aztecs). This site contains a wealth of information on the Aztecs, including an excellent illustrated overview of their unique, myth-based religious festival, the Fire Ceremony.

Fall of the Aztecs, PBS (www.pbs.org /conquistadors/cortes/cortes_flat .html). Part of a PBS documentary on the Aztecs and how they were conquered by the Spaniards.

Huitzilopochtli, *Myths Encyclopedia* (www.mythencyclopedia.com/Ho-Iv /Huitzilopochtli.html). The online *Myths Encyclopedia* offers this overview of the Aztec sun god and his role in Aztec mythology; includes numerous links for more information.

Quetzalcoatl, *Myths Encyclopedia* (www.mythencyclopedia.com/Pr-Sa /Quetzalcoatl.html). A very informative site about the Feathered Serpent deity, who played a major role in the Aztec myth about the creation of humanity.

INDEX

Q

Q, the Winged Serpent (film), 83
Quetzacoatalus (pterosaur), 84–85, *85*
Quetzalcoatl (Feathered Serpent), *8,* 8–9
    Aztec agriculture and, 20–21
    bas-relief of, *36*
    birth story of, 32
    in creation myth, 33–34
    myth of predicted return of, 9–12
    in popular culture, 82–84

R

Religious ceremonies, 39

S

Sahagun, Bernardino de, 22, 59
Servant of the Underworld (Bodard), 81
A Soldier in Every Son (Moncada), *80,* 81
Stargate SG1 (TV program), 83
Sun gods, 30, 35

T

Tamoanchan (mythical paradise), 56
Techichi dogs, 45–46
Tecuciztecatl (god of seashells), 38, 40
Templo Mayor (Greater Temple), *26*
Tenochtitlan (Aztec capital), 13–14, 18,
    25, 70, *70,* 71
    Diego Rivera's mural of, *79*
Teotihuacano people, 15, 18
Tezcatlipoca (Smoking Mirror), 8, *8,* 9, *17,*
    22, 31, 36, 77
    in creation myth, 33–34

destruction of Toltecs and, 16–18,
    28
    in popular culture, 82
    as sun god, 35
Tlaloc (rain deity), 15, 26, 34, 35–37,
    55
    as sun god, 35–37
Tlalocan (mythical paradise), *54,* 55
Tollan (Toltec capital), *16*
Toltec people, 9, 15–16
    demise of, 16–18, 22, 28
Topiltzin Quetzalcoatl, 9
Trek (TV program), 82–83

U

Utes (Indian tribe), 63

V

Virgin of Guadalupe, 78

W

Water Sun age, flood destroying, 31,
    44–45, 77
Wind Sun age, 35

X

Xipe Totec (creator god), 30, 32
    in creation myth, 33–34
Xitle volcano, 42
Xochiquetzal (goddess), 31, 34, 36, 77
Xolotl (Quetzalcoatl's dog), 48–49, *49,*
    78

ABOUT THE AUTHOR

Historian Don Nardo has written numerous acclaimed volumes about ancient civilizations and peoples. Among these are studies of the religious beliefs and myths of those peoples, including the Sumerians, Egyptians, Persians, Greeks, Romans, Celts, and others. Nardo also composes and arranges orchestral music. He resides with his wife, Christine, in Massachusetts.